TERRORISM

Perspectives from the Behavioral and Social Sciences

Panel on Behavioral, Social, and Institutional Issues
Committee on Science and Technology for Countering Terrorism

Neil J. Smelser and Faith Mitchell, *Editors*

Center for Social and Economic Studies

Division of Behavioral and Social Sciences and Education

NATIONAL RESEARCH COUNCIL
OF THE NATIONAL ACADEMIES

D1597845

THE NATIONAL ACADEMIES PRESS
Washington, DC
www.nap.edu

THE NATIONAL ACADEMIES PRESS
500 Fifth Street, NW • Washington, DC 20001

NOTICE: The project that is the subject of this report was approved by the Governing Board of the National Research Council, whose members are drawn from the councils of the National Academy of Sciences, the National Academy of Engineering, and the Institute of Medicine. The members of the committee responsible for the report were chosen for their special competences and with regard for appropriate balance.

International Standard Book Number 0-309-08612-4

Additional copies of this report are available from

The National Academies Press
500 Fifth Street, NW
Box 285
Washington, DC 20055
800/624-6242
202/334-3313 (in the Washington Metropolitan Area)
<http://www.nap.edu>

Suggested citation: National Research Council (2002) *Terrorism: Perspectives from the Behavioral and Social Sciences.* Panel on Behavioral, Social, and Institutional Issues, Committee on Science and Technology for Countering Terrorism. Neil J. Smelser and Faith Mitchell, editors. Division of Behavioral and Social Sciences and Education. Washington, DC: National Academies Press.

THE NATIONAL ACADEMIES
Advisers to the Nation on Science, Engineering, and Medicine

The **National Academy of Sciences** is a private, nonprofit, self-perpetuating society of distinguished scholars engaged in scientific and engineering research, dedicated to the furtherance of science and technology and to their use for the general welfare. Upon the authority of the charter granted to it by the Congress in 1863, the Academy has a mandate that requires it to advise the federal government on scientific and technical matters. Dr. Bruce M. Alberts is president of the National Academy of Sciences.

The **National Academy of Engineering** was established in 1964, under the charter of the National Academy of Sciences, as a parallel organization of outstanding engineers. It is autonomous in its administration and in the selection of its members, sharing with the National Academy of Sciences the responsibility for advising the federal government. The National Academy of Engineering also sponsors engineering programs aimed at meeting national needs, encourages education and research, and recognizes the superior achievements of engineers. Dr. Wm. A. Wulf is president of the National Academy of Engineering.

The **Institute of Medicine** was established in 1970 by the National Academy of Sciences to secure the services of eminent members of appropriate professions in the examination of policy matters pertaining to the health of the public. The Institute acts under the responsibility given to the National Academy of Sciences by its congressional charter to be an adviser to the federal government and, upon its own initiative, to identify issues of medical care, research, and education. Dr. Harvey V. Fineberg is president of the Institute of Medicine.

The **National Research Council** was organized by the National Academy of Sciences in 1916 to associate the broad community of science and technology with the Academy's purposes of furthering knowledge and advising the federal government. Functioning in accordance with general policies determined by the Academy, the Council has become the principal operating agency of both the National Academy of Sciences and the National Academy of Engineering in providing services to the government, the public, and the scientific and engineering communities. The Council is administered jointly by both Academies and the Institute of Medicine. Dr. Bruce M. Alberts and Dr. Wm. A. Wulf are chair and vice chair, respectively, of the National Research Council.

www.national-academies.org

PANEL ON BEHAVIORAL, SOCIAL, AND INSTITUTIONAL ISSUES

Contents

Preface

To stress the salience and urgency of the national situation as dictated by contemporary terrorism and to underscore the need for behavioral and social science understandings of that situation are to pronounce the self-evident. Terrorism, already recognized by some as the looming form of international conflict in the late twentieth century, moved dramatically to center stage on September 11, 2001, and promises to occupy national attention for decades. It is also evident that while the scientific, technological, and military aspects are essential parts of understanding and containing terrorism, every aspect of that phenomenon yields human and social dimensions. This report has the objective of bringing behavioral and social science knowledge and understandings to bear on terrorism and the responses to it.

Shortly after the September 11 attacks, the presidents of the National Academies, comprising the National Academy of Sciences, the Institute of Medicine, and the National Academy of Engineering—wrote a letter to President George W. Bush pledging the scientific resources of the nation, as represented in the National Academies, to help contend with the new national crisis. As part of that pledge the Academies established the Committee on Science and Technology for Countering Terrorism, which began work immediately and issued a comprehensive report on the relevance of science and technology for defending the nation against terrorist activities.

As part of its work the committee spun off eight panels on specialized aspects of terrorism, some of which are preparing their own reports. The group responsible for this report is one of these panels. Two of our panel members served as members of the main committee, and many parts of our report have been incorporated into the master report. However, the report contained in these pages was prepared independently of the work of the larger committee.

In this report we focus first on the nature and determinants of terrorism itself and, second, on domestic responses to terrorist activity. Under the first heading we take up nettlesome definitional issues, and then—moving from remote to proximate determinants—consider the international, demographic, economic, political, and cultural determinants of terrorism, as well as its motivational and organizational aspects.

Under the second heading we bring knowledge about disaster behavior to bear on the topics of preparedness, warning, and short-term responses to terrorist attacks, calling attention to likely longer-term political, economic, and cultural processes of recovery. At the end we present our best sense of the priorities for behavioral and social science research on many aspects of terrorism.

The panel included scholars from the disciplines of anthropology, demography, economics, history, political science, psychology, and sociology. Its special areas of expertise include the history of Muslim societies, the contemporary Middle East, the politics of the state, revolutionary social movements, deterrence and game theory, the cognitive structure of beliefs, disaster studies, the politics of diplomacy and peacekeeping, and social change. The panel met twice in Washington, DC, on January 13-14 and February 24, 2002. Between the meetings the panel members undertook drafting assignments and exchanged materials and ideas by email. We pooled our general knowledge of relevant topics, read what we deemed as the best in the exploding literature on terrorism, and made use of the face-to-face meetings to synthesize as best we could the extremely diverse strands of knowledge at our disposal. The report that follows represents a solid consensus on the part of the panel.

The panel would like to thank the National Research Council staff who supported our work and facilitated the achievement of this ambitious goal: Faith Mitchell, study director; Janet Garton, program associate; and Benjamin Woolsey, project assistant. Erik Smith worked as a consultant with Eugene Hammel on new demographic analysis. Lewis Branscomb, Richard Klausner, and other members of the main committee made helpful comments about the draft and provided other intellectual contributions. The panel is grateful as well to the National Academies for their financial support.

This report has been reviewed in draft form by individuals chosen for their diverse perspectives and technical expertise, in accordance with procedures approved by the Report Review Committee of the National Research Council. The purpose of this independent review is to provide candid and critical comments that will assist the institution in making its published report as sound as possible and to ensure that the report meets institutional standards for objectivity, evidence, and responsiveness to the study charge. The review comments and draft manuscript remain confidential to protect the integrity of the deliberative process.

We thank the following individuals for their participation in the review of this report: Phillip Heymann, Harvard Law School; Alex Inkeles, Hoover Institution, Stanford University; Edward H. Kaplan, School of Management, Yale University; Clark McCauley, Psychology Department, Bryn Mawr College; Henry Riecken, University of Pennsylvania School of Medicine (emeritus); and Edward Wenk, Jr., Emeritus Professor of Engineering, Public Affairs and Social Management of Technology, University of Washington.

Although the reviewers listed above have provided many constructive comments and suggestions, they were not asked to endorse the conclusions or recommendations nor did they see the final draft of the report before its release. The review of this report was overseen by Robert Frosch, Belfer Center for Science and International Affairs, Harvard University, and Charles Tilly, Departments of Sociology and Political Science, Columbia University. Appointed by the National Research Council, they were responsible for making certain that an independent examination of this report was carried out in accordance with institutional procedures and that all review comments were carefully considered. Responsibility for the final content of this report rests entirely with the authoring committee and the institution.

Neil J. Smelser, *Chair*
Panel on Behavioral, Social, and
Institutional Issues

Executive Summary

The events and aftermath of September 11, 2001, profoundly changed the course of history of the nation. They also brought the phenomenon known as terrorism to the forefront of the nation's consciousness. As it became thus focused, the limits of scientific understanding of terrorism and the capacity to develop policies to deal with it became even more evident. The objective of this report is to bring behavioral and social science perspectives to bear on the nature, determinants, and domestic responses to contemporary terrorism as a way of making theoretical and practical knowledge more adequate to the task. It also identifies areas of research priorities for the behavioral and social sciences.

· ·

NATURE OF TERRORISM

The panel adopted a general approach to the phenomenon, moving beyond—but including and focusing on—the vivid but historically specific image of stateless, religiously based terrorism that animates the Al Qaeda and similar operations. (We have, however, largely left out of consideration perhaps the greatest source of terrorism of this time—the terrorization of an established government against its own citizens.) A search for precise *general* definitions of terrorism yielded a multiplicity of overlapping efforts, some more satisfactory than others, but none analytically sufficient.

In surveying the scene, the panel came up with a working definition that is satisfactory for most purposes. It includes the ingredients of (a) illegal use or threatened use of force or violence (b) with an intent to coerce societies or governments by inducing fear in their populations (c) typically with political and/or ideological motives and justifications and (d) an "extrasocietal" element, either "outside" society in the case of domestic terrorism or "foreign" in the case of international terrorism.

At the same time, terrorism emerges as what is called an "essentially contested concept," debatable at its core, indistinct around its edges, and simultaneously descriptive and pejorative. The panel suggests approaching terrorism not as a discrete thing, but rather in terms of a number of discrete dimensions, which combine and recombine in various manifestations of terrorist activity.

· ·

DETERMINANTS OF TERRORISM

Terrorism is multiply determined, with a diversity of remote and proximate determinants nesting together in combination to produce the resultant patterns of activity. Moving from longer-term to shorter-term levels, the following range of determinants emerge:

Regions most likely to produce terrorist threats have a long history of *international relations*—economic, political, and cultural—with the West, including more recent phases of colonialism and economic and cultural penetration in the accelerated process of globalization. Many current terrorist ideologies single out American political and economic policies as objects of their opposition. This imparts a distinctive political cast to contemporary international terrorism, establishing its kinship with other forms of international conflict.

Among the *impacts* of these relations of international domination are economic and political dislocation, new religious and secular values, and the emergence of new economic classes and political groups, including those that form around the issue of either modernizing or preserving traditional ways of life.

Most non-Western societies, including Muslim societies, are disadvantaged in *demographic and economic* respects. Demographically, they are located in the high-fertility, high-growth regions of the world. These patterns produce substantial demands on countries' resources and yield a population pyramid with many young and few elderly, resulting in high youth dependency ratios. These in turn put adverse pressure on education systems and produce large numbers of unemployed youth with dim economic futures and high potential for dissatisfaction. Economically, many of these countries are both poor and have highly regressive distributions of income but at the same time have been exposed to high economic expectations, not least in the Western media.

In *reaction* to these international, demographic, and economic circumstances, these societies become resentful—more precisely, ambivalent—toward outsiders held responsible for their plight. Among the social movements that arise are those inspired by a revivalist ideology, which is characterized by a profound sense of threat to traditional values and society, an abiding hatred for agents held responsible (mainly foreigners), and a vision of restoration of their own societies to a state of traditional purity. These movements provide a sense of meaning for the disaffected and an explanation for their plight. They have also provided a fertile seedbed in which terrorist organizations can find both recruits and sympathetic audiences for their activities.

From a *political* point of view, revivalist movements tend to appear in countries ruled by regimes that repress even legitimate forms of political opposition. Such repression tends to drive these movements underground and radicalize them. While much of contemporary terrorism is "stateless"—organized in far-flung organizational networks that are relatively unreachable—terrorist organizations must maintain certain political relations with the states in which they are harbored, and these may constrain their activities.

From the standpoint of *individual psychology*, the panel concludes that there is no single or typical mentality—much less a specific pathology—of terrorists. However, terrorists apparently find significant gratification in the expression of generalized rage, in the sense of identity imparted by membership, and by the glamour derived from carrying out actions before real and imagined audiences. The group processes involved in the recruitment, induction, and training of terrorists are extremely powerful motivating forces.

From the standpoint of *social organization*, terrorists operate mainly through elusive networks that are constrained simultaneously to maintain extreme secrecy and to coordinate complex military-like activities, as well as to sustain a high level of ideological commitment among members. These characteristics reveal a number of strengths as well as vulnerabilities, among which are defection, internal power struggles, and schismatic tendencies.

DOMESTIC RESPONSES TO TERRORISM

Our guidelines for proper anticipation, preparedness, and warning systems are drawn from knowledge based mainly on situations of natural disaster, but modified in light of what is known about terrorist threats. In addition, we sketch a scenario of short-term disaster-like responses. This sketch includes possibilities of catastrophic disaster, which includes not only massive death and destruction, but also breakdowns of social order and resultant group conflict.

Behavioral and social science research has revealed the following processes involved in long-term recovery:

Processes of *normalization* following attacks—diminution of emotional responses and return to familiar activities, events, rhythms, and conflicts—all reversible in the event of repeated attacks. In connection with normalization, the insights provided by two relatively new avenues of research in the behavioral and social sciences—cultural trauma and collective memory—are promising for understanding the longer-term reactions to September 11 and other potentially massive events.

Possible *political consequences* of concerns with national security. Among these are the compromise of civil liberties, group scapegoating, muting of political opposition, and extremist political movements.

Likely *economic consequences*, including the dislocation and redirection of economic emphasis, costs of rebuilding, capitalizing on public crisis for private economic gain, disputes over who pays for readiness, damage and recovery, episodes of economic instability, and possible downgrading of domestic economic programs and environmental concerns.

SOME RESEARCH PRIORITIES

Cognizant of the inadequacies of the knowledge base about both the history and contemporary manifestations of terrorism, the panel identifies and elaborates a number of priorities for research in the behavioral and social sciences. Eleven of these concern research on terrorist characteristics: their background and motivations ; types of terrorist organization; terrorists' choice of targets; terrorists' audiences; the political, economic, demographic, and cultural contexts of terrorism; and improving databases. Seven of the priorities concern research on responses to terrorism: warning systems; immediate reactions to terrorist attacks by affected communities and response agencies; longer-term political, economic, and cultural developments after terrorist events; and the scientific and political significance of ethnic profiling.

1 Clearing the Conceptual Air

The catastrophic events and aftermath of September 11, 2001, have been so dramatic that they have led to the understandable conclusion that the world has entered an "age of terrorism." People have experienced terrorism—by whatever definition—for centuries if not millennia, and there is increasing consciousness of the phenomenon, especially in the past three decades. Nevertheless, since September 11 consciousness of terrorism has taken a quantum leap. Contemporary terrorism now looms as a new and menacing situation without end, calling for new approaches on many fronts, including a new kind of preparedness and a new kind of struggle against it. In this report we intend both to confirm and to qualify this impression of novelty.

Even prior to the recent, supercharged attention to terrorism and terrorists, social scientists had difficulty grasping these phenomena analytically. A summary account of terrorism, published on the eve of September 11, complained that "terrorism is a contested concept that resists precise definition," that it is not "a central element in major theories of war and conflict," that it is difficult to "make comparisons or draw general conclusions," and, above all, that "there is no comprehensive unifying theory of terrorism" (Crenshaw, 2001, p. 15605). We intend to qualify this gloomy diagnosis by bringing behavioral and social science knowledge to bear on many aspects of contemporary terrorism.

The operative passages in the charge to the panel on Behavioral and Institutional Issues (called here the DBASSE panel) read as follows:

> The purpose of the DBASSE panel is to provide guidance on terrorism-related behavioral, social, and institutional issues to the federal government. It will operate under the aegis of a National Academy of Sciences-wide committee, the Branscomb-Klausner

Committee on Science and Technology for Countering Terrorism. . . . The panel is charged with writing a report that will include (1) a typology of terrorism; (2) an evaluation of the current state of knowledge and capacity for dealing with the most significant threats; and (3) a research agenda.

The DBASSE panel responded to this charge and prepared this report in the context of two closely related additional activities. The first is the panel's contribution to the work of the parent Branscomb-Klausner Committee. Two of the panel members, Neil J. Smelser and Thomas C. Schelling, were members of the parent committee. That committee's report is entitled *Making the Nation Safer: The Role of Science and Technology* (National Research Council, 2002). Chapter 9 of that report, "The Response of People to Terrorism," contains much of the material in the "responses to terrorism" section of this report, and behavioral and social science contributions appear in many other parts of that report as well. Readers will note that the research recommendations in Chapter 9 of *Making the Nation Safer* are not identical to the recommendations in this report. These differences reflect the different authoring bodies, whose perspectives on research priorities were not uniform.

The second line of activity is a report by the National Research Council's Panel on Understanding Terrorists in Order to Deter Terrorism, sponsored by the Defense Advanced Research Projects Agency (DARPA). That panel had the same chair as the DBASSE panel, and eight individuals were members of both panels. The DARPA panel concentrated more narrowly on the issues of what terrorists value and what kinds of sanctions, inducements, and policies can be brought to bear in influencing those valued elements. Its report is entitled *Discouraging Terrorism: Some Implications of 9/11* (National Research Council, in press). Taken together, the materials in the three reports constitute a significant compilation of available behavioral and social science knowledge relating to terrorism, brought together in the period following September 11, 2001.

As the reader will appreciate, the charge to the DBASSE panel is extremely broad and permissive ("to give guidance on terrorism-related behavioral, social, and institutional issues") and left the panel with great discretion with respect to what issues it would pursue. Furthermore, the parent committee gave full freedom to the panel to develop the report in any directions it chose.

Before sketching how we responded to the three subparts of the charge, we should point out that up to the present, the behavioral and social sciences—like many other lines of inquiry—have not focused much research on the characteristics of terrorists, the organization of terrorist activities, or the determinants of terrorism. We do not claim to know the reasons for this relative neglect, but among them are its relative unfamilarity as a form of warfare, its analytic slipperiness (see the discussion on definitions and typology below), and the fact that most terrorist activity, designed to be carried out in secret and done so if it is successful, yields a very skimpy supply of available empirical data. In recent months, of course, a river of research on terrorism has begun to flow, and a full torrent of concerned but nonscientific writing has appeared. All these circumstances have dictated that the two panels (DBASSE and DARPA) did what was possible in consulting research directly on terrorism, but also went to different and related research topics, such as disaster studies, the literature on social movements, deterrence analysis, and some work on international economic and political relations.

The DBASSE panel dealt with the subelements of the charge in the following ways:

(1) We addressed the issues of definition and typology directly. However, instead of being able to locate an authoritative definition already "out there" empirically, we found that no such satisfactory general definition could be found in the conceptual haze surrounding the literature on terrorism. We did develop a working definition that provided a guide for us, but we also went beyond and analyzed the unsatisfactory state of definitional affairs. We also decided to identify a number of dimensions of terrorism, along which its variations can be described and which yield the tools for a provisional number of types, rather than seeking a typology from the array of empirical phenomena that have been termed terrorism.

(2) We decided to organize the "state of knowledge" about terrorism by assembling our best understandings of the diverse manifestations and determinants of the phenomenon, as well as its consequences. However, our report does not claim to cover all the available and relevant research literature; rather, it focuses on material germane to the main line of the panel's argument. In addition, we acknowledge that the current state of

knowledge does not provide bases for formulating specific and unequivocal responses to terrorist threats. We trust that following through on the panel's proposed research agenda will improve that knowledge base.

In fact, there are important topics related to terrorism that the panel was not able to take on. These include an examination of technological advances that change the costs and benefits of terrorism as a strategic choice; terrorism and its deterrence as a signaling game with imperfect information; the role of the media, especially in the Middle East; and terrorism, and support for it, as a diffusion process at the level of social groups.

The panel also did not consider questions of responsibility for failures of intelligence, did not address such political questions as the types of trials appropriate for apprehended terrorists, or provide policy advice.

(3) We produced 18 research priorities arising from our substantive analyses. These are found at the end of the report.

DECODING THE MYSTERY OF TERRORISM: NEW OR OLD, FAMILIAR OR UNFAMILIAR?

Especially after the attacks on the World Trade Center and the Pentagon—but also in response to some earlier attacks—a vivid but very oversimplified conventional wisdom has developed about the contemporary terrorist threat. It portrays that threat as both new and unfamiliar. The following are the relevant ingredients of that view:

• Most purposive human activities are directed toward reducing uncertainty in the environment as a means of coping with that environment. The aims of terrorist activities are to create, maximize, and continuously shift the parameters of uncertainty, confusion, insecurity, and fear.

• The evolution of terrorism from World War II—through the phases of colonial struggles, hostage-taking, hijacking, assassination, explosive bombing, and suicidal vehicle and airplane bombing—shows a certain mercilessness in the perpetration of violence: any target, at any time, in any place, and by any means. The overriding premium is on quickness, surprise, shock, and generating reactions of horror and terror.

• Contemporary terrorism is often stateless and not territorially bounded. It operates largely in the form of territorially fluid networks that are relatively unreachable politically and diplomatically.

• The contemporary terrorist mentality and culture, which are rooted in absolutist, either-or, good-and-evil world views, resist efforts to negotiate, because accommodation, bargaining, and mutually acceptable compromise are not envisioned as possibilities within many terrorists' mental framework. A leading Islamic terrorist proclaimed that "God does not negotiate or engage in discussion." In a similar vein, the former leader of Hezbollah stated, "We are not fighting so that the enemy recognizes us and offers us something. We are fighting to wipe out the enemy" (quoted in Hoffman, 1998, pp. 98, 96). A corollary of terrorism based on absolute religious principles is that it is resistant to mechanisms of peaceful influence and persuasion, to say nothing of conversion, because of the strength and rigidity of these principles.

• This absolute, noncontingent mentality frequently stands side by side with other characteristics that can only be described as rational and adaptive: a sharp sense of reality and reality testing, inventiveness, maneuverability, ingenuity, and instrumental capacity that has been manifested in terrorist planning and execution of attacks.

• Known military solutions can neutralize specific terrorist organizations and can reduce the probability of terrorism in the short run, but they cannot suppress or destroy the cultural and motivational forces that inspire terrorism. These forces are the complex result of cultural definitions, historically generated hatreds, international power relations, contemporary economic and social conditions, and doctrinal education. In the worst-case scenario, military defeat may intensify some of the forces generating terrorism. In all events, the limitations of military conquest bring to mind the analogy that a one-time weeding of the garden can be only a short-term solution.

• The same can be said of the effects of economic sanctions against terrorism, such as blocking financial assets, choking off imports and exports, and assaulting the drug trade. These may achieve the same short-term results as military action does, but even successful economic action does not suppress and may aggravate the forces that generate terrorist activity.

In this report we hope to demonstrate that this composite view, while plausible in many respects in assessing the present international terrorist situation, is likely to be myopic with respect to every one of the characteristics listed. In fact, every "constant" in the above description turns out to be a variable.

In addition to its own internal variability, contemporary terrorism shares some characteristics with a number of other types of historically known situations. Terrorist groups themselves call forth a number of other phenomena with which limited comparisons can be made:

- crime and disorder, both domestic and international (e.g., the international drug trade),
- guerilla warfare,
- social banditry,
- cults, sects, witchcraft and satanic groups, suicide clubs,
- extremist social movements, and
- sociopathic behavior.

Reactions to terrorist situations and attacks call to mind:

- plagues and famines,
- natural and accidental disasters (e.g., floods, fires, storms, earthquakes, and major industrial accidents),
- wartime life,
- episodes of intense international crisis (e.g., the Cuban missile crisis of 1962), and
- prolonged periods of international tension (e.g., the cold war).

Terrorism is like every one of these, but it is identical to none of them. One can therefore learn from all of them, but new understandings and modes of coping with the historically unique situation currently facing the nation and the world are needed.

ISSUES OF DEFINITION

In the panel's search for an adequate definition of terrorism, we came upon a paradoxical—and to some degree, paralyzing—result. There are several ingredients of this result: (a) A proper definition of terrorism is an essential ingredient in understanding the phenomenon and in crafting responses to it. (b) Actual definitions are multiple, varying greatly in inclusiveness. (c) A reasonable but necessarily imperfect working definition is, however, possible. (d) The term "terrorism" is a stigmatizing concept; as a result, definers, labelers, and the labeled are eager selectively to exclude themselves and their own actions under the term and, correspondingly, to include others and their actions under it; the result is that "terrorism" is a politically contested concept. (e) Given this frustrating set of circumstances, a reasonable strategy is to abandon the search for the one, true definition of terrorism and (f) rely on a strategy of identifying relevant dimensions of terrorism, highlighting one or more of these according to its usefulness in understanding a given problem and in the interest of maximizing flexibility of responses to an obviously multifaceted phenomenon. We comment briefly on each of these ingredients.

THE NEED FOR DEFINITION

A working definition of terrorism is necessary because the government must respond to it in unambiguous and legal ways, and citizens and others—including the international community—must recognize those responses as legitimate and not capricious. A scientific and analytical approach may guide the government toward the adoption of definitions and policies that are operationally most useful.

There are three major dangers in erroneous definitions of terrorism. First, defining it too broadly will dilute and waste resources that could be put to more efficient preventive and defensive use. Second, a too broad definition may catch in its net persons not at all engaged in undesirable activity and may violate their constitutional rights or international conventions. Third, defining terrorism too narrowly means that people will not be protected from unanticipated kinds of attacks. In principle, terrorism must be defined both sufficiently and efficiently.

ATTEMPTS AT DEFINITIONS

We attempt no comprehensive survey of definitions (Johnson, 2001; Ruby, 2002) but give a few to indicate their variations in scope and their problems. One writer commented, "A universally recognized definition will be elusive. One survey of leading academics revealed 109 different definitions of what constitutes 'terrorism'" (Takeyh, 2002:70).

A simple and straightforward definition is that terrorism consists of acts designed to induce terror. True to the name of the phenomenon, it nevertheless includes a world of behaviors in which we are not practically interested (e.g., stalking and sadistic "mind games").

Another brief definition is found in the *Merriam-Webster Collegiate Dictionary*: "the systematic use of terror, especially as a means of coercion." This includes a broader intent, contained in the word "coercion," but it also leans in the direction of vagueness and overinclusiveness.

In 1988 the State Department issued a definition of terrorism: "premeditated, politically motivated violence perpetrated against noncombatant targets by subnational groups or clandestine state agents, usually intended to influence an audience" (U.S. Department of State, 1988). This is a helpful definition, but the terms "politically motivated," "noncombatant" and "subnational" seem unduly constrictive, given the known diversity of motives, targets, and organizational modes of terrorism.

The *American Heritage Dictionary* contains a more elaborated definition: "unlawful use or threatened use of force or violence by a person or an organized group against people or property with the intention of intimidating or coercing societies or governments, often for ideological or political reasons." Is not "unlawful" perhaps too constricting and "threatened use of force" too inclusive?

WORKING DEFINITION

In these definitions there are recurring definitional characteristics: illegal use or threatened use of force or violence; an intent to coerce societies or governments by inducing fear in their populations; typically with ideological and political motives and justifications; an "extrasocietal" element, either "outside" society in the case of domestic terrorism or "foreign" in the case of international terrorism. These ingredients provide a useful composite, which the panel has used as a practical guide. However, neither singly nor in combination do these ingredients provide an unambiguous and uncontestable definition. We now proceed to say why this is so.

CONTESTATION

For nearly half a century, philosophers and linguists have written about what is called an "essentially contested concept" (Gallie, 1956). The main idea is that some concepts are inherently incomplete, without being totally incoherent, and are filled out differently by individuals and groups who bring different backgrounds, beliefs, and political convictions to bear on them. Moreover, the meanings of such words change in emphasis over time. Words that have been named as falling into this category are "work of art," "democracy," "rape," "poverty," and "underclass."

Terrorism seems to be such a word. It is a concept with great rhetorical power but limited scientific precision. What is "terrorism" to some may be called "freedom fighting" by others. Ambiguity as to what is to be included under the concept at its borders poses another conceptual difficulty. As an exercise to demonstrate these features of contestation, we ask the reader to scan the following list and try to determine which of them are terrorist acts and which are not (or, perhaps better, who would call each terrorism and who would deny it):

- British and American firebombing of Dresden in World War II
- Dropping atomic bombs on Hiroshima and Nagasaki in World War II
- Sherman's march through Georgia during the American Civil War
- Palestinian suicide bombing
- Israeli punitive strikes on Palestinians
- Lebanese Phalangist militia attacks on Muslims
- The Bay of Pigs

- Project Camelot
- Haganah and Irgun attacks on the British in Palestine
- The original Sicilian Mafia as an organization to protect the peasants
- Organized crime, especially protection rackets
- Lynchings, church bombings, and Ku Klux Klan activities generally
- International drug trade and the financing of guerillas
- The "reign of terror" in postrevolutionary France
- Stalin's purges of the 1930s
- Ruby Ridge
- Waco
- Frank and Jessie James

Not only are many of these acts ambiguous but the arrays of phenomena classified as terrorism differ according to the definition chosen. This exercise alone should demonstrate the havoc that essentially contested concepts wreak on attempts to be scientifically precise in defining the term.

TERRORISM AS A SET OF DIMENSIONS

One productive way to come to terms with these definitional conundrums is to forsake the effort to conceive of terrorism as a thing to be defined and, instead, to seek out a number of dimensions along which terrorist and quasi-terrorist activities fall. This exercise may or may not yield a definite typology, but in any event it provides a basis for avoiding historical and comparative myopia and considering the variability and complexity of terrorism and its fluidity of organization over time. Having understood these features, we may be in a position to make more intelligent and focused decisions about how to contend with it.

One of the more elaborate attempts to lay out dimensions is that of Schmid et al. (1988), who identify 10 common bases for classifying terrorism: (1) actor based, (2) victim based, (3) case based, (4) environment based, (5) means based, (6) political orientation based, (7) motivation based, (8) demand based, (9) purpose based, and (10) target based. Still other bases could be imagined. As a further exercise in thinking dimensionally, we produced a dimensional analysis, overlapping with that of Schmid et al., based on the questions: Who are the actors? What are their actions? And what are the consequences of these actions? Each of the categories contained in these questions is broken down further, yielding the ingredients of a complex typology as well as a number of derived types. The results of this exercise, as well as some of its implications, are found in Appendix A.

The panel sees several potential advantages to this kind of dimensional thinking: it offers a more open-ended approach to the range and complexity of terrorist behavior than a single, fixed definition; it provides an avenue for disentangling the problems of meaning we have identified; and it provides the basis for developing a systematic comparative analysis of different manifestations of terrorism.

2 Origins and Contexts of Terrorism

As seems inevitable, when ambiguous and alarming events occur and unfold, many single and oversimplified explanations appear, and these represent, in part, attempts to reduce uncertainty and anxiety. Thus, the causes of terrorism suggested include "poverty," "inequality," "globalization," "technology," "energy," "oil," "Islam," "Islamic fundamentalism," and "psychopathy," among others. There are also widespread challenges to each of these causes on both scientific and ideological grounds.

In approaching the daunting questions of origins and contexts we are guided by the following first principles:

• The search for a single or even a few causes is misguided. The factors influencing contemporary terrorism are a blend of historical, economic, political, cultural, motivational, and technological factors, to name only the most obvious.

• The logic of cause-followed-by-effect is inappropriate to the understanding of origins and contexts of terrorism. Causes differ qualitatively in their generality as determinants. Some are remote background conditions, others are facilitating circumstances, others are precipitating factors, and still others are inhibitory factors. The most appropriate way to organize these factors is in a nesting or combinatorial way. Each adds its value at a different level and significance to work toward more complete accounts and explanations.

• At the very least it is essential to separate the origins and context issue into two distinguishable levels: (a) the historical, social, political, and cultural conditions that constitute a favorable soil in which terrorism can take root and grow, provide a continuously changing mix of support and discouragement for terrorism, and constitute one of the main audiences for terrorists and (b) the immediate motivational, ideological, group, and organizational determinants of terrorist activities themselves. The explanations at each level are separate, though they overlap and articulate with one another as one regards the total picture. We employ this distinction in our own account, treating the more general conditions first and the immediate ones afterward.

· ·

IMPERIALISM, COLONIALISM, AND GLOBALIZATION

The impulse for territorial expansion, conquest, and domination is as old as history itself. The ways in which this impulse has expressed itself, however, reveal vast differences. For comparative purposes, we mention three variations.

Imperialism is, above all, a system based on military conquest, territorial occupation, and direct governmental/military control by the dominant imperial power. This characterization clearly applies to the classical Roman, Ottoman, Spanish, and Soviet empires, and it is also evident but not so unequivocal in other cases, such as the Austro-Hungarian Empire. The political sovereignty of occupied regions is not a salient issue; that notion does not apply to militarily occupied and controlled territories. Imperial powers are also dominant economically, but the mechanisms are extraction and exploitation of resources through the mechanisms of expropriation, direct control of economic activities, and coercion (including slavery in some cases).

If we regard the eighteenth-, nineteenth-, and twentieth-century European cases as the major referents, *colonialism* overlaps with but is distinguishable in important ways from imperialism. Military conquest, settlement, territorial acquisition, and administrative rule—sometimes military, sometimes civil—is the essence, but in practice the administrative rule varied from direct rule resembling imperialism to indirect rule involving a symbiotic relationship between colonial rulers and indigenous authorities. Nineteenth- and twentieth-century colonialism also involved more striking economic contrasts between the technological and industrial superiority of the (developed) colonial powers and the (undeveloped) colonial countries. The resultant pattern was the extraction of primary products necessary for industrial production (e.g., cotton from India and Egypt) or for consumption in the colonizing countries (e.g., tea, sugar, coffee, spices).

After the effective demise of British, French, Dutch, and Belgian colonialism in the decades after World War II, there was acceleration in the development of the form of international organization described as *globalization*. Globalization is something of a misnomer, because economic, political, and cultural penetration around relevant parts of the globe is observable through several millennia. Since the collapse of the Soviet bloc in 1989-1990, the world system has also been called "the American hegemony." This is also misnamed, because the dominant powers are a complex combination of North American, West European, and East Asian powers. Nevertheless, the role of the United States is paramount. The contemporary global mode is one of economic influence, realized through greater economic productivity (and its concomitant, wealth) based on a superior, science-based technology. This influence is realized and exercised by the mechanisms of trade among nations, capital and financial investment, and power in the international monetary system.

There is also an aspect of military domination, but this is primarily realized not through military conquest and administration of occupied territory, but through a technologically superior arsenal of weaponry, occasional wars and "peacekeeping" interventions, and, above all else, military intimidation. American hegemony also has a less tangible political-ideological ingredient, namely, a conviction of the moral superiority of a particular (American) version of democracy and its accompanying characteristics of personal liberty, constitutional rights of citizens, and mass political participation. This ideological dimension affects U.S. foreign policies toward other nations, generally favoring nations like itself politically and distancing itself from or applying pressures on nations unlike itself. The final aspect is a cultural one, consisting mainly of the effective export of cultural and materialist values through the worldwide American domination of the mass media, especially television.

In that part of the world that currently commands the nation's special attention—referred to variously as the Arabic or Islamic world—we observe a long period of interaction, penetration, and conflict with the West. Especially in the late eighteenth century, there was exposure to and borrowing of Western military and other technology and such ideas as democracy, nationalism, and the rights of women, as travel, commercial activity, and communication increased. The forces of modernization, however they may be defined, are thus several centuries old; an informative account of the historical process is found in Lewis (2002). Of special subsequent significance was the century-long (1830 through the end of World War I) colonization and political control of North Africa and the Near East countries of Syria, Lebanon, and modern Iraq, Jordan, and the Palestine mandate. In the twentieth-century, commercial and cultural penetration and influences have accelerated, dramatically in the case of the exploitation of oil but more generally as well.

• •

IMPACTS ON "RECEIVING" SOCIETIES

The general impacts of the complex of influences imposed by more powerful societies are both to dislocate and to provide alternatives to the traditional ways of life in the affected societies. Economic production is transformed, systems of wage-labor increased, existing patterns of inequality altered, economic expectations stirred, and political institutions modified or displaced. Traditional and authoritarian political values and institutions are shaken by exposure to ideas of freedom, rights, and democracy. Competing religious forces, especially nonreligious secularism, are introduced. And especially recently, commercial and cultural penetration has exposed the world, and notably the non-Western world, to a range of materialistic values and aspirations that are evidently unattainable in those societies in the historical short run.

A political corollary of these modernizing influences is that, under conditions of domination by and acculturation to a more powerful society, the receiving society experiences an increase in the growth, complexity, and magnitude of political divisions. Some of these are "class" in nature, as new groups—for example, a new middle class, a paid laboring class, or the unemployed—come into being and develop interests in common. Other divisions are cultural in nature, as groups crystallize along the dimension of how much and in what ways they want to be modernizers (e.g., democratic, capitalistic, secular) and how much and in what ways they want to preserve a traditional way of life.

All these impacts are observable in dramatic form in the world's Islamic societies. They combine with several additional features of these societies to make for very high levels of discontent and combustibility.

Almost all of the Islamic societies in the world fall into the category of rapidly growing populations that have relatively high proportions of young people compared with those of working age, but low proportions of elderly people. The Muslim population is the most rapidly growing religiously defined category in the world, doubling perhaps every 25 years at current rates. These populations have been growing on an average of more than 3 percent per year, although fertility is declining in many of them (Roudi, 2002). These patterns yield large families in which younger siblings in particular are likely to suffer from lack of parental investment of resources and emotional care.

Such societies have few resources to devote to education, so their high numbers of young people cannot be trained to participate in advanced economic activities. It is hard for such countries to guarantee employment for their youth, who experience high rates of unemployment, engage in criminal activity or gang violence, or must otherwise migrate to the richer countries, where they work in low-level jobs. Such poor countries are also often obliged to spend substantial sums on police control and national defense against neighboring poor countries, in which they employ local youth in low-level military jobs.

The majority of the world's Muslims are poor and live in countries characterized by great inequalities of wealth (World Bank, 2002). The ratio of children to workers in the Muslim world is very high, especially because there are so few women in the labor force, so the actual ratios of children to workers are almost double the child to adult ratio. Finally, high growth ratio produces large numbers of children in families, and this may spread thin the family's financial and emotional resources. Some research suggests that later-born children in families are more rebellious. This suggests the possibility that in a population in which many families have many children, the level of rebelliousness in the society may be higher (Sulloway, 1996; Skinner, 1992; Paulhus et al., 1999; Zweigenhaft and Von Ammon, 2000).

The relevance of these outcomes to an understanding of

social unrest is clear. Unemployed young males with poor local prospects will feel angry and frustrated. They can seek a future in military endeavors, emigrate to take menial work, or become involved in criminal activity in a foreign and often culturally inhospitable environment. Sexual frustration may also be part of the picture. Marriage is often a high-cost matter in these countries because it requires substantial outlays for parents and elaborate ceremonies. Young women have restricted choices in the local marriage market because of the male exodus and little hope of employment themselves unless they also emigrate (especially if local customs deter them from entering the labor market).

Looking at these demographic and economic realities, it is clear that the majority of Muslims in the world experience a high level of absolute poverty. These poor compare themselves with the rich in their own societies and with an unrealistic view of Western culture gleaned from films and television, and thus they also experience a high level of relative deprivation. This combination is a sure recipe for social unrest in general. Insofar as these conditions are blamed on the United States and the West in general—as they typically are—they also provide a favorable atmosphere for supporting violence against these enemies, as well as a potential recruiting ground for recruits to this cause. To note this is not to argue that poverty causes terrorism, but that it is one ingredient in a volatile mix of causes.

• •

REACTIONS TO IMPACTS

It is a reasonable historical generalization that those who are dominated—or who believe themselves to be dominated—by stronger outside powers come to resent and oppose their oppressors. Especially under conditions of imperialist and colonial domination, in which direct force is used against the population, this discontent can often be held in check, at least temporarily. When societies experience economic and cultural domination without direct military occupation and political control, the opportunities to express discontent publicly are usually more readily available.

This rejection of outside domination is not surprising and can be readily appreciated. It is not as frequently appreciated that the hatred of outside domination is typically only half the picture. The other half is conveyed by the idea of *ambivalence*.

To bring the point closer to home, anticolonial ideologies are mainly negative toward the colonial powers. But they also contain the seeds of positive attraction. A remote but telling instance of this is found in the cargo cults, a widespread religious phenomenon mainly in colonial Melanesia. These movements, which were millenarian, envisioned the end of the world accompanied by the arrival of Western ships or airplanes loaded with tinned foods, transistor radios, and other Western items. At the millenarian moment, too, white Westerners would be destroyed, and the true believers would survive in a world of Western plenty (Worsley, 1957). Further evidence of this type of ambivalence is provided by the fact that colonial societies, once independent, frequently establish institutions and retain political and other values resembling those of their former conquerors.

A similar ambivalence toward the United States is now found throughout the world, including (perhaps especially) Muslim societies. On one hand there is America the demon, the rich, godless, morally and sexually corrupt, imperialist country that has come to its wealth by exploitation, a power that dominates the world and forms alliances with the ruling elites in their own societies, a nation that is hypocritical in its assertions of equality when it is plagued with racism and poverty, and the power that is primarily responsible for the existence and support of Israel. Side by side with this, however, is a utopian America, as the immigrant communities of Detroit, Brooklyn, and Los Angeles typify. America is a place to come to, a place of wealth and consumption where the payoff for hard work is leisure and opportunity, and where freedom is buttressed by myriad choices in both the market and in the polity. This positive side of the ambivalence, moreover, stands in stark contrast to what almost all Muslims can realistically aspire to in their own societies.

Typically, it is psychologically difficult to hold both sides of an ambivalent attitude at the same time, and it usually is resolved by rigidly accentuating one side to the exclusion of the other. In anti-American Muslim ideologies this appears to be the case, with vitriolic hostility as the conspicuous and exclusive element and the admiration and envy suppressed. Insights that take account of this element of ambivalence signal a potential chink in the armor of what appear to be exclusively hostile attitudes, yield a more realistic grasp of the social psychology of protest and resentment, and instruct Americans as to the half-truth of the question asked by some in the wake of September 11: "Why do they hate us so much?"

• •

CULTURAL CONTEXT

The complex of economic, political, and cultural penetration does not occur in a vacuum. It is always interpreted and reacted to in the framework of the cultural milieu it affects—accepted, altered, synthesized, or rejected, all in complex ways. An inevitable accompaniment of the process is the widespread perception that the domestic culture is under threat of extinction. The reactions to this perception are, as indicated, multiple, but, in light of the religious character of much of recent terrorism, we take special note of what have been called revivalist or fundamentalist reactions. This variant of terrorism in particular has developed in the context of a wider Islamic revival.

Revivalist or fundamentalist movements are efforts to restore an often-imagined indigenous culture, especially its religion, to a pure and unadulterated form. Their elements have been found in American Indian movements such as the ghost dance (Mooney, 1896) and peyote religion (Slotkin, 1956), revivalist cults, nationalist movements in colonial societies, revivalist and fundamentalist Christian movements, and in some extreme Western political movements such as fascism. The typical ingredients of such movements are:

- A totalistic worldview rooted in a sacred religious system.
- A profound sense of threat, angst, and apprehension about the destruction of their society, culture, and way of life.
- A specification of certain agents who are assigned total responsibility for this deterioration.
- An unqualified, and absolute, sense of rage that is felt to be morally legitimate.
- A utopian view of their own culture and society—perhaps referring to an imagined, glorious past—standing in

point-by-point opposition to the decaying and threatening world they confront (Smelser, 1962: 120-29; Juergensmeyer, 2000).

The historical picture in many Muslim societies is not different from this general pattern. The analogy is not between cults and terrorism as such, but between nativistic movements and Islamic revivalism, which provides a fertile ground for religiously based terrorism. The penetration of Muslim societies by Western values during the past few centuries has occurred in the context of Islam, one of the world's great religions, dedicated to the transcendence of God and the observance of Islamic law. It is also a religion with a proselytizing tradition and a centuries-long history of both conquest of and humiliation by Western Christian and Eastern Orthodox powers—a history actively remembered in detail in Muslim societies to this day. It is, finally, a religion with a keen sense of infidels, both inside and outside Islam. All these features have conditioned the reactions to the West in Muslim societies, including the Islamic revival.

Revivalist-like movements of a totalistic sort—i.e., to "Islamize" the religious community by imposing Islamic norms throughout all spheres of life—antedate deep Western influences. Among these are the Safavid movement that eventually became the basis of the Shiite state in Iran. There were also a number of nineteenth-century antecedents, and the early twentieth century witnessed the rise and consolidation of the Muslim Brotherhood in Egypt and its subsequent underground offshoots (Voll, 1994).

The widespread Islamic revival in contemporary times partakes of elements of these earlier movements but has added new and different ingredients (Maddy-Weitzman, 1996). Some of these ingredients include: (a) It expresses the feelings of humiliation at the loss of the supremacy of Islam, the imposition of European commercial and colonial power, and the Euro-American domination in world affairs. Its enemies are foreign infidels, non-Muslims in their midst, representatives of more moderate forms of Islam, and secular dictatorial regimes in their own societies. (b) It expresses a fear of cultural extinction by the spread of an American consumerist lifestyle, and of individualistic values disrespectful of the old hierarchies of society. (c) It typically takes hold in countries ruled by regimes that repress even legitimate forms of domestic political opposition (Abootalebi, 1999).

On the more constructive side, the goal of the revivalist movements is the creation of an ideal Islamic society, in which morals are pure and the community just, and all live in a state that protects a Muslim way of life, defends it against enemies, and aggrandizes the domain of Islam. Revivalists regard this envisioned society as a comprehensive alternative to nationalism or capitalism. In the main, the movements are carried by self-declared charismatic teachers, ideologues, community organizers, and political activists. The followers are diverse, consisting of petit bourgeois *bazaaris* (small businessmen, peddlers, craftsmen, and workers) and *maktabis* (clerks, teachers, and students) and sometimes the professional middle classes (McCauley, in press; Library of Congress, 1999; Maddy-Weitzman, 1996; Hamzeh, 1997; Sivan, 1997; Abootalebi, 1999; Alam, 2000). The movements have become extensively institutionalized in schools, mosques, clinics, study groups, women's auxiliaries, and economic enterprises. Some groups take the form of political lobbies and parties, and some have paramilitary forces (Hamzeh, 1997). They constitute opposition movements to domestic governments, as in Turkey, Egypt, Algeria, and Indonesia, or to foreign rulers or occupiers, as in Palestine, Chechnya, Xinjiang, and Kashmir (Sivan, 1997; Alam, 2000).

The revivalist movements represent a small part of Islam in general. It is not difficult to appreciate, however, why Muslim terrorists have taken on the ideology of militant revivalism as their major guiding belief system. It provides a meaningful account of what is wrong in their world and legitimizes their extreme and violent political actions. To say this is neither to assert that Islam "causes" terrorist behavior nor to say that terrorists are simply "exploiting" Islamic beliefs to rationalize their destructive ends. Rather, the presence of extreme Islamic fundamentalism, like the demographic, economic, and political realities found in most Muslim societies, is part of the fertile seedbed in which a particular ideologically based brand of terrorism finds a supportive audience and some recruits. We emphasize, however, that Islam-inspired terrorists are a minority of terrorists, considered worldwide, and that the vast majority of Islamic peoples have no connection with and do not sympathize with terrorism; this relationship is represented in Figure 2-1.

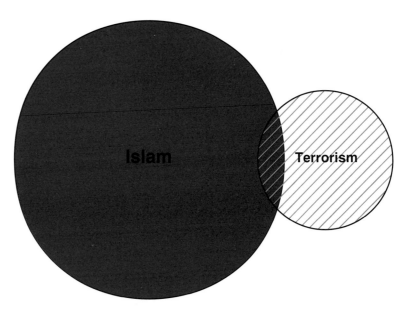

FIGURE I   Islam and Terrorism*
*Indicative only: Not to scale

• •

STATELESSNESS AND STATES

Recent terrorist activity in general and the particular organization of Al Qaeda have cemented the view that the "new terrorism" involves a distinctive asymmetry: a stateless and nonterritorially bounded organization that wages war against a state, and vice versa. In domestic terrorism the terrorist organization typically operates within a state but itself is not a state. In international terrorism, the organization may operate within the confines of a single state, but it typically involves a far-flung organization or network of organizations, operating out of the territories of whatever states will harbor, tolerate, or cannot detect it. Corollaries of this view are: (a) that these organizations are out of range of institutions of truce, international diplomacy, alliances, and treaties, all of which are peaceful alternatives to warlike violence; (b) that, unlike states, these organizations do not face the "conservatizing" influences imposed by the state's necessity to maintain law and order and manage politically negotiated relationships among diverse groups (except in the most totalitarian of societies, and to a limited degree in these); and (c) that they are relatively unreachable militarily because they are moving and semivisible targets, forever changing their form and moving from state to state and from place to place within states. This view contains much truth, but it must be qualified in two ways: first, that all "states" are not states as we understand them, and, second, that the relations between states and terrorist organizations are highly variable.

The standard Western model of a state is that it is a discrete, territorially bounded, politically sovereign unit with a legal monopoly over force and violence, responsible for law and order in its domestic population, and the focus of the solidarity, culture, and identity of its citizens. Regarding the panoply of states and other organizations in the contemporary world, we must conclude that the state is not a unitary thing that is either present or absent but is a continuum. The West still has many states that approximate the model—despite the intrusions of globalization on all states—but Afghanistan, Algeria, Colombia, Rwanda, Somalia, Sudan, the former Yugoslavia, and Zaire, while in the United Nations as states, do not, for various reasons, meet the understood conditions. Much has been made recently of the notion of "failed states" to describe the nondevelopment of modern states in the non-Western (including the Muslim) world in the political science literature (Zartman, 1995; Rubin, 2002). Finally, many "nonstate actors" take on state-like roles—United Fruit in Honduras, Aramco in Saudi Arabia—as did the East India Company in an earlier era of British colonialism.

In addition, whatever their approximation to the standard model, states have variable, not fixed, relations with terrorist networks. At one extreme there is the Taliban, which had supportive, hand-in-glove relations with Al Qaeda. Pakistan has had a vacillating relationship with terrorist organizations. Egypt has allowed their terrorists to leave to fight as terrorists in other places but curtailed their activities radically at home. Finally, when Libya at its inception entered the United Nations as a state, it had almost no attributes of a state and has only slowly developed those characteristics. Its international capriciousness during the first two decades of the regime of Muammar al Qaddafi—including some "state terrorism"—drew military attacks from the United States and sanctions from the international community. Since the end of the cold war, Libya has evolved more toward statehood and membership in the world of states. No longer a pawn in the cold war and facing internal threats from Islamic opposition groups, Libya is not now considered a major part of the worldwide terrorist threat and, indeed, actively collaborated with the United States in the wake of the September 11 attacks.

To realize this double variability—of states themselves and of state-terrorist relations—is at one level heartening. Since all states maintain some kind of relations with terrorist organizations if they are in their midst—supporting, neglecting, opposing, suppressing—this means that foreign policy exercised through state-state relations has variable potential to operate as one form of constraint, albeit uncertain, against terrorism and terrorist activities.

MOTIVATIONS FOR TERRORISM

We now shift from an emphasis on the broader origins and contexts of terrorism to individual terrorists in their group and organizational settings. We have already touched on background reasons for supporting or joining terrorism, such as economic desperation, political repression, and the ready presence of a framing religious ideology. We now turn to more immediate psychological motives, while fully aware of the slipperiness of this exercise. The perils are that (a) human variation is such that there is no single, "typical" terrorist psychology; (b) many terrorists are psychologically inaccessible and when accessible often secretive and nonyielding; and (c) Western psychological concepts and assessments often are not readily exportable and applicable to cultures very different from their own.

INDIVIDUAL MOTIVATIONS

With respect to motivational profiles, work by Jerrold Post and others has suggested some similarities among members of given terrorist organizations, as well as some differences among the prototypical membership of different organizations. For instance, members of the German Red Army Faction and the Italian Red Brigades were likely to come from broken homes, and members of the Basque ETA group have come disproportionately from mixed Spanish-Basque parentage. "Comparable data are not available for Shi'ite and Palestinian terrorists, but specialists share the impression that many of their members come from the margins of society and that belonging to these fundamentalist and nationalist groups powerfully contributes to consolidating psychosocial identities at a time of great societal instability and flux" (Post, 1990: 31). In all events, generalizations of this sort must always be tempered by the recognition that the composition of terrorist organizations is diverse and that well-educated and wealthy individuals are also represented, particularly in leadership ranks. More recent research on terrorists has rejected the idea that psychopathy is a key feature of terrorist motivations (McCauley and Segal, 1987; Ruby, 2002; Crenshaw, 1981; Post, 2001).

Leaving aside considerations of pathology or normality, the identity conferred by participating in a terrorist organization can be quite glamorous and appealing. As Post observed about one youthful recruit of a terrorist organization, "Before joining the group, he was alone, not particularly successful. Now he is engaged in a life and death struggle with the establishment, his picture on the 'most wanted' posters. He sees his leaders as internationally prominent media personalities. Within certain circles he is lionized as a hero" (Post, 1990: 36).

Glorification of and personal salvation through violence is not limited to Islamic terrorists. Salvation as a voluntary martyr to violence or suffering has a religious history with roots in the theology of Christianity, Judaism, and Islam, as well as analogs in Buddhism. It is only because terrorists and their source populations on one hand, and target populations on the other, *share* these cultural precepts that such acts have the psychological impact that they do. Self-fulfillment through perpetration of violence also has a history, going back at least to nineteenth-century anarchists, early elements of Soviet communism, and some elements of the cowboy culture. Similarly, utopian visions achieved through apocryphal transformation are not limited to Islam but are common both in mainstream and sectarian aspects of Christianity and Judaism. They are also found in cultures outside the province of the three major Near Eastern religions, although it is not always clear that they have appeared entirely independently of their influence (examples are Melanesian cargo cults and the ghost dance of American Indians).

The glamour of the terrorist identity depends to a large extent on the terrorists' success. For example, following the tremendous media attention accorded the Palestinian cause in the wake of the killing of Israeli athletes at the Munich Olympics by the Black September faction of the Palestine Liberation Organization, thousands of Palestinians rushed to join the terrorist organizations (Hoffman, 1998:74). It is evident that joining a terrorist group is not related uniquely to any given motivational profile. The search for identity is probably important, but so is the venting of anger, the power motive, and the glamour and aura of heroism and martyrdom—all operating in the context of situational opportunities.

INSTILLING TERRORIST OBJECTIVES: THE PROCESS OF BECOMING A TERRORIST

Why do individuals relinquish the societal values they have been brought up to cherish and adopt an extremist value system that may condone the killing of innocents? Studies of brainwashing, religious conversion, cults, as well as of terrorist groups per se provide a likely answer. It has to do with extreme forms of group influence and social pressures for conformity. The objectives are to isolate the individual from other belief systems, to delegitimize and dehumanize potential targets, to tolerate no uncertainty in rejecting or even killing skeptics, and to adore a leader. All these, taken together, create a separate, closed-minded social reality at variance with the social reality of origin or the social reality of alternative cultures.

As Ehud Sprinzak notes: "Ideological terrorism does not emerge from a vacuum or from an inexplicable urge on the part of a few unstable radicals to go berserk. . . . In the main, the process does not involve isolated individuals who become terrorists on their own because their psyche is split or they suffer from low esteem and need extravagant compensation. Rather, it involves a group of true believers. An understanding of this group process seems to be much more important than an understanding of individual terrorists' personal psychology" (1990: 78). Once in the grasp of the group, it matters less what motivation may have brought the individual there in the first place (McCauley, in press).

An extreme illustration of this process is suicide bombing. Ariel Merari, an empirical investigator of suicide terrorism in the Middle East and Sri Lanka, writes (personal communication, January 10, 2002):

> The key to creating a terrorist suicide is the group process. Terrorist suicide is an organizational rather than an individual phenomenon. To the best of my knowledge, there has not been a single case of suicide terrorism which was done on the suicide's personal whim. In all cases, it was an organization that decided to embark on this tactic, recruited candidates, chose the target and the time, prepared the candidate for the mission, and made sure that he/she would carry it out (often via a back-up detonation device activated via remote control in case the would-be terrorist got cold feet after all). The three critical elements in the preparation are boosting motivation, group pressure (e.g., mutual commitment), and creating a point of no return (public personal commitment) by videotaping the candidate declaring that he is going to do it and having him write last letters to family and friends.

TERRORISM AS A PUBLIC PHENOMENON

One intrinsic objective for terrorists is the drawing of attention to themselves or their cause, not only among their supportive constituencies but also from the whole world. News of terrorists in the media and in public awareness is omnipresent. It is inconceivable to think of a public event—the Olympics, an economic summit, any official gathering—without worrying about security and the threat of terrorist activity. The amount of publicity and literature devoted to terrorism in the past six months is unprecedented. Osama bin Laden was a contender for *Time* magazine's "Man of the Year" status, which was ultimately awarded to New York Mayor Rudolph Giuliani. The basis for inclusion was related to terrorism in both cases.

The tremendous attention-getting potential of terrorism may have given rise in the 1990s to a new brand of terrorism that Ehud Sprinzak (2001) recently called "the megalomaniac hyperterrorist," by which he means "self-annointed individuals with larger-than-life callings: Ramzi Youssef (the man behind the 1993 World Trade Center bombing), Shoko Asahara (leader of Aum Shinrikyo and architect of the 1995 gas attack in Tokyo subway station), Timothy McVeigh (the 1995 Oklahoma City bomber), Osama bin Laden (likely planner of the September 11 carnage)," Igal Amir, who assassinated Itzhak Rabin—all manifesting in some degree a desire to use catastrophic attacks in order to write a new chapter in history.

Whereas attention-getting in and of itself may be gratifying to terrorist leaders, successful terrorism sometimes advances terrorists' real-world objectives. High-casualty suicidal terrorist attacks on U.S. and French targets in Lebanon contributed to the decisions of those countries to withdraw their forces. Hezbollah, or the Party of God, is regarded in Lebanon (nearly universally) as the successful vanquisher of the Israeli occupation. Perhaps not coincidentally, 18 months after the slaughter of the Israeli athletes in Munich, Yasser Arafat was invited to address the UN General Assembly. Attention to Islam and Muslim values and traditional Islamic ways is on the rise among young generations of Muslims worldwide. The interest in Islam as a culture is rising, and the call for reexamination of U.S. foreign policy in regard to Muslim countries is no doubt related to attention that terrorist attacks have drawn to these issues.

• •

ORGANIZATION OF TERRORISM: NETWORKS

The preferred organizational form for terrorism is organizational networks or, perhaps better, networks of network-based organizations (Arquilla and Ronfeldt, 2001; Kerbs, 2001). Like other aspects of terrorism these networks are relatively unfamiliar to those who study organizations, who have focused more on formal organizations, such as corporations, hospitals, universities, civil service bureaucracies, voluntary organizations, and organizations that direct the activities of social movements. As a result, there are only some, mainly indirect insights about terrorist organizations from the literature on formal organizations (Crenshaw, 1987).

The characteristics of terrorist organizations can be understood by tracing out the implications of the fact that terrorism must be simultaneously invisible and at the same time coordinated for preparing and executing terrorist activities. Consistent with these purposes, terrorist organizations must maintain extreme secrecy, avoid record-keeping, and minimize any paper trails that could reveal their internal movements, plans, and intentions. The last is extremely difficult to ensure completely, because of the necessity to rely on computer and telephone—in addition to handwritten and face-to-face—communication as a part of organizational coordination, and the necessity to rely on financial transaction institutions to shift resources from place to place and on credit cards to facilitate movements of their personnel by cars, buses, trains, and airplanes.

The foreign affairs or external political exigencies of terrorist organizations are limited and concern mainly their relations with the host states in which they are located. If they are unknown to those states—rarely if ever the case—then questions of foreign relations with them are moot, because terrorist organizations avoid routine interactions with governing regimes. However, host states usually know about, tolerate, protect, or promote terrorist organizations for their own political purposes. This means establishing relations with terrorist organizations, taking an interest in and perhaps influencing their activities, thus forcing the terrorist organizations to observe and perhaps play along with various state-related realities (Crenshaw, 1985).

Because much of the glue of terrorist organizations is commitment to an extreme ideology in a group with extreme solidarity, this generates a special range of issues of maintaining internal control. They must recruit those whom they regard as ideologically committed and ideologically correct. While there have been news reports that claim to trace associations between individual terrorists and specific schools or other social ties, the panel is not confident that these purported ties are sufficient evidence to make conclusive statements.

Regardless of where recruits come from, the leaders must dedicate some of their organizational activities to maintaining that loyalty and commitment and preventing backsliding among members who are frequently living in societies with values, ways of life, and institutions that are different from their own and may be found seductive. The need to maintain various kinds of discipline through intense personal ties, hierarchical control, and surveillance is very strong. Organizations must ensure that information flows but also that it is kept secret. They must coordinate extremely complex activities of destruction. And they must ensure steadiness of ideological commitment (Della Porta, 1992).

There are several associated points of vulnerability of terrorist organizations, many of which involve failures of information flow, security of information, and coordination of activities.

One additional vulnerability, characteristic of all ideologically extreme and rigid organizations, is the constant danger of schismatic ideological tendencies from within (Schiller, 2001). Demanding extreme conformity, such organizations constantly face problems of internal deviation, mutual accusations among both leaders and followers that they are less than true believers, the splitting off of factions based on ideological differences, and the political intrigues that are involved in preventing such splits and dealing with them once they have occurred (Ansell, 2002).

Direct knowledge about these organizational dynamics is very frail, mainly because it is so difficult to study organizations that are bent on secret operations and concealment of information. Such knowledge must usually come from defectors, detainees who cooperate, and agents who have been able to infiltrate. However, the world has experienced many other kinds of secret, network-based organizations, and a base of knowledge about them and their operations has accumulated (Kerbs, 2001). Among these organizations are spy networks, gang rings such as the Mafia, drug-trafficking organizations, Communist cells, sabotage operations undertaken during wartime and during the cold war period, and extremist social and political movement organizations. In addition, network analysis as a field of study in sociology, social psychology, and elsewhere has yielded a great deal of theoretical and empirical knowledge during recent decades, and some aspects of this general knowledge might also be brought to bear. See, for example, the work of Carley (2001).

We conclude this long section on origins, contexts, motives, and organization of terrorism by noting a number of potential limitations on and vulnerability of contemporary terrorism: (a) their partial dependence on "domestic" friendly audiences, whose support and applause can wane if the terrorists appear to be inept or gratuitously excessive in their activities; (b) their dependence on states within which they operate—variable in terms of their precise relationship with those states—which may constrain their activities in light of their own "state" interests in the international arena; (c) extreme ideological/religious rigidity and backsliding, both of which have the potential to generate schisms within the terrorist organizations; (d) motivational failings, reversals, and defections, always a possibility when so much psychic energy is invested in an extreme cause; and (e) organizational failures, especially in flows of information in a dispersed, secretive network.

3 Responses to Terrorism in the United States

The targets of terrorist attacks are multiple and diverse. This fact constitutes an advantage for terrorists, because it is one facet of the uncertainty on which they capitalize—where and when will an attack occur and what kind of attack will it be? Some targets of terrorist attacks are human beings themselves, for example, assassinations, the bombing of large human assemblies, and biological and chemical poisoning and contamination. Others do not attack humans at all but aim to disrupt some vital economic or institutional functioning, for example, disruption of financial institutions or computer networks. No matter what the attack, however, there is always a human *response* to it. In this chapter we summarize much of what is known about these responses from research in the behavioral and social sciences.

. . . .

ANTICIPATION, PREVENTION, PREPAREDNESS, AND WARNING

Throughout its history, the American nation has been relatively free from anxieties about attacks on its homeland, except for a few wartime situations (including the cold war). The "age of terrorism," however, with us for some time but dramatically imposed by the events of September 11, has led to a heightening of multifaceted anxiety. This is especially difficult to dispel, largely because of the irreducible quotient of uncertainty involved. A condition of high anxiety, moreover, leaves a population skittish and prone to extreme reactions, mainly rumors and exaggerated fears.

Preventive measures may be sought at five points in the

terrorist process: (a) long-term efforts to modify the demographic, economic, political, and cultural background of terrorism; (b) prevention at the source, that is, by seeking out and disrupting terrorist activities—in the present case, in staging areas in the several countries that knowingly harbor terrorists and to some extent in countries that do not wish them there; (c) prevention at the end of the line, by erecting defenses at the locus of known or conceivable targets, such as dams, public buildings, mass assemblages of people, and so on; (d) along the way between source and event, by controlling the movements of people and weapons at the national borders and other points of entry; and (e) after an attack, by having in place a response-and-recovery apparatus that will minimize its effects.

A few comments on the middle three measures are in order. On one hand, the attractiveness of the at-the-source alternative is that, if successful, it prevents all sorts of terrorism. On the other hand, intelligence and military operations of this sort are very costly and constitute a significant drain on the nation's resources; it is also impossible to ensure that eradication efforts will ever approach anything like completeness, given the secrecy and mobility of terrorists and their networks. In addition, even if eradicated, terrorist activities and organizations can regrow. Finally, aggressive ferreting poses certain perils of unilateralism and the peeling away of allies and friends if the pursuit appears to them to be too aggressive.

The attractiveness of along-the-way strategies is similar in that they intercept persons with a possible diversity of purposes, but in this case as well, both the cost and the impossibility of completeness are evident, given the mass movement of things and people that global commerce and tourism entails. The attractiveness of the end-of-the-line strategy is security but, given the multiplicity of targets and the adaptive capacity of terrorists to change them and invent new ones, it also raises the questions of cost and the impossibility of completeness. Considerations of strategic prudence and the force of national public opinion probably dictate that the country will pursue all three lines of prevention.

Preparedness for attacks should be organized at two levels—responsible authorities and the general population. At the level of government and community officials, preparation should be both exhaustive and contingent—anticipating every kind of attack, understanding the probable ripple effects, thinking in terms of multiple attacks, preparing proper responses for agents who give out information in crisis situations, detailing the roles of first-line response agencies such as police and rescue agencies, and developing a whole range of backup responses to contain damage and minimize future damage. These measures will also call for new levels of cooperation among government, the media, schools, businesses, hospitals, churches, and other types of organizations, as well as households. Applied research, conducted in advance, on all these aspects of preparedness is necessary.

At the level of the populace the effort is both educational and instructional. As much unambiguous information as possible should be disseminated about the nature of different kinds of attacks—information that is clear, placed in context, repeated, and authoritative (Mileti et al., 1990). Training and drills for behavioral responses for each generally increase the sense of mastery and reduce anxiety before the attack and reduce both chaos and human death and suffering in the event of attack. Readiness and preparedness involve a number of delicate equilibria, however. If attacks do not occur for a long period of time, public apprehension diminishes and knowledge about responding properly erodes. Recall the high-profile, sometimes hysterical movement to protect against fallout in the wake of a nuclear attack in the 1950s and 1960s. Despite encouragement by both government and the media, only 1 in every 100,000 people actually built some sort of fallout shelter (*New York Times*, "Week in Review," Dec. 23, 2001, p. 12). The desired equilibrium is to keep public consciousness high without whipping up public anxiety. Overtraining and overdrilling, moreover, can generate public indifference, irritability, and criticism of responsible authorities.

Warning systems also create a delicate balance. Authorities should strive to make warnings free from ambiguity, directed to all those at risk (wherever they may be), and communicated through multiple channels (public warning devices such as sirens, radio, television, and Internet) (National Science and Technology Council, 2000). False alarms and misdirection of warnings to people not at risk, however, tend to generate public apathy and hostility (Dow and Cutter, 1998).

DISASTER-LIKE RESPONSES TO ATTACKS

Behavioral and social science research carried out mainly, but not exclusively, during World War II (U.S. Strategic Bombing Survey, 1947) and the civil defense era of the 1950s and 1960s (e.g., Wallace, 1956) yields a reliable store of knowledge about behavior during and after disaster situations. We detail below a typical scenario:

- An initial response of disbelief, denial, and emotional numbing.
- A wildfire spread of information, both factual and fictional (mainly rumors) as a part of the process of comprehending and assigning meaning to the events; much of this is by word-of-mouth and telephone (if possible), but over time the mass media have taken over a decisive role in the structuring of cognitive and emotional reactions.
- The appearance of a mix of intense emotional reactions, including fear, anxiety, and terror, as well as rage, guilt, grief, and serious mental disturbances in a small proportion of the affected population; some research (Wolfenstein, 1957) indicates that many of the extreme reactions occur among individuals already suffering from mental disorders.
- The occurrence of a mix of collective behavior reactions, such as rare episodes of collective panic (Quarentelli, 1977), rapid movement of people in an effort to join and help loved ones, some disorganized behavior, and some "derived" behaviors, such as looting and crime in the context of a temporary breakdown of social order. Research on hurricane disasters has shown that, even when warned, households make their own assessments of risk and actively decide whether or not to evacuate, depending on such factors as level of risk perceived, job circumstances, concern for personal property, and family situation (Dow et al., 1999; Dow and Cutter, 2000).
- A rush to the scene of a disaster ("convergence effect") of agencies formally designated to respond to crisis situations (police, firefighters, and military personnel, as well as rescue and relief agencies), along with individual and group rescue activities; at the same time, the occurrence of failures of communica-

tion and coordination in these responses, as well as some conflict and jurisdictional squabbling among the agencies. One of the most common vulnerabilities of responses to disaster is the uncertainty of mission and communication among different response agencies (Tierney et al., 2001: 47-54).

• The development of a notable social solidarity, including a pulling-together of the affected community to respond to the crisis; altruistic and heroic behavior; an increase in trust of other individuals, groups, and authorities; an augmented spirit of cooperation and good will; and the spread of euphoric feelings as a kind of collective offset to the negative emotional responses.

• The simultaneous appearance of scapegoating reactions, directed primarily at individuals believed to be responsible for permitting the disaster to occur and for failures in responding to the crisis.

• A gradual return to the routine and the normal, including the management and diminution of intense affective reactions by way of adaptive processes akin to mourning; the restoration and recreation of broken social ties, a return to familiar rounds of activities, and the completion of recovery and reconstruction efforts.

In the aftermath of the catastrophic events of September 11, 2001, every one of these ingredients appeared. Yet limited comfort can be taken from these observations and insights, because the contemporary terrorist situation, as it has evolved, does not correspond to "normal" disaster reactions. It is more complex than these, calling for a correspondingly increased complexity in efforts to comprehend and respond to it.

To begin with the most basic differences, terrorism involves intended and manipulated disasters, as contrasted with acts of God and accidental misfirings in complex systems of industrial, transportation, and economic organizations. This element of deliberateness, moreover, involves maximizing the surprise, uncertainty, novelty, and diversity of assaults, thus limiting the effectiveness of discrete efforts to anticipate, prepare for, and respond to single types of terrorist attacks. The contemporary terrorist situation thus dictates that one abandon any conception that there is a single and unified disaster syndrome and incorporate complexity, contingency, and continual adaptation and revision of thinking about, readying for, and preventing terrorist events and situations.

As we now understand it, terrorism involves great variations along the following, overlapping lines:

- Discrete types of targets, including buildings, food and water supplies, electrical and other energy systems, transportation systems, information and communication systems, large human populations (including bombings as well as chemical and biological poisoning), currency and financial systems, and governmental structures.
- Degree of localization (e.g., explosion) or dispersion (e.g., biological contamination) of assault.
- Degree to which targets are symbolically charged (railroad tracks at one extreme, sacred symbols such as the Statue of Liberty at the other).
- Whether attacks are single or multiple.
- Whether attacks are one-time or recurrent, and if recurrent, how erratic or "random" in pattern.
- Whether the agent of attack is known, suspected, ambiguous, unknown, or unknowable.

As should be evident from this listing, the mix and multiplicity of responses in the ideal-typical disaster syndrome is highly variable. Localized attacks, especially if they involve the closing of escape routes, are more likely to occasion collective panic reactions. Generalized attacks, such as contamination and poisoning, are likely to cause reactions of mass hysteria but not localized panics. Widespread terror—a generic objective of terrorist attacks—is more likely to occur when attacks are dispersed, multiple, unpredictably recurrent, and by ambiguous or unknown agents. And converging rescue and relief operations are qualitatively different for localized bombings than they are for attempts to poison or sicken large numbers of people. Finally, the mix of reactions will differ widely according to whether human casualties result from the attack and whether the attack is immediately recognizable or is perceived as having invisible or unknown dimensions.

It is instructive to comment on the September 11 attacks on the World Trade Center and the Pentagon in this context. Widespread terror was not the most salient feature of the immediate response to the events. Rather, September 11 created an intense reaction of moral outrage against a readily identifiable and "evil" enemy and a reaction of exceptional collective resolve to unite, mobilize, and retaliate—violently and with perceived legitimacy—against that enemy. In that limited sense, the attacks present an appearance of miscalculation. (The sense of uncertainty created by the assaults, however, has generated a persistent level of anxiety in the population.) As such, the September 11 attacks, like Pearl Harbor 60 years earlier, were a "natural" for American society and national character—which includes a sense of ambivalence and inhibition in initiating aggression but a great capacity to respond morally and collectively when unequivocally provoked by an act of aggression from outside (Mead, 1965 [1942]).

Some insights about the anthrax mail episode a few weeks later can be generated as well. As passing and amateurish as those events seemed to be, they nevertheless had a potential to be very terror-inducing. This lay in the many kinds of uncertainty surrounding the episodes. The agents were unknown. The fatal effects of widespread exposure could be extensive. And mail, like currency, is something that everyone regularly handles. The episode left room for feelings of danger for everyone—that it could strike anywhere, any time—however unrealistic such fears may have been. The press also played a role, scarcely deliberate, in magnifying the threat, bringing what were essentially a series of highly localized events to the attention of a vast population of viewers and readers.

• •

NORMALIZATION

As indicated, the natural history of recovery from disaster involves a diminution of emotional responses, the setting in of a certain denial of the possibility of recurrence, and a return to routine activities, events, rhythms, and conflicts. These are, by and large, reasonable and adaptive responses on the part of a population because of the rarity of specific kinds of catastrophic events in life. It is not psychically economical for people to worry about them all the time.

Discrete acts of terrorism, if not soon repeated, should be expected to show the same tendency toward routinization. Indeed, there were messages from government and public leaders exhorting the public to return to normal activities in the wake of the September 11 attacks, while at the same time stressing the need for vigilance and even warning of impending attack.

Should additional major attacks on the homeland occur, the whole routinization process would be thrown in the air and a new situation created. Many of the emotional and behavioral symptoms of the disaster syndrome would recur, but in a different context of public memory of the earlier attacks. Scapegoating of governmental and other agencies and persons singled out as lax or irresponsible would become more salient because of expectations that vigilance and security should have increased as a result of the previous attacks. Subsequent attacks would also probably lead to even more tightening of homeland security, along with all the psychological and political consequences that would ensue. If, down the line, a dreadful scenario of multiple, repeated, and continuous terrorist attacks should unfold, one would expect the emergence of, among other things, a certain routinization of disaster reactions, including an inuring and hardening of public outlooks and behavior reminiscent of what has been witnessed over time in places like Northern Ireland, Israel, and Lebanon.

Because the attacks of September 11 were such a dramatic and profound wound to the nation, they qualify as what social scientists and humanists recently have been calling a cultural trauma. Within a matter of days after the assault, it was appreciated in all quarters that these events would embed themselves deeply in the nation's memory and endure indefinitely. Unlike some other cultural traumas that are mainly negative—regicides and assassinations of national leaders, holocausts, and episodes of ethnic cleansing—September 11 already emerges not only as a deep scar on the nation's body, but also as a moment of extreme heroism and pride. In the wake of the events, the nation has simultaneously experienced both deep mourning and a not altogether expected season of celebration.

A cultural trauma of this type can be expected to manifest a number of known characteristics:

• The event is indelible, not only not forgotten but unable to be forgotten;
• It is sacred, not in any specific religious sense, but as a monumental instant in the history of the nation;
• There are deliberate efforts to remember the event and its heroes collectively, through commemorative ceremonies, pub-

lic observation of anniversaries, and the erection of monuments; and

• There is sustained public interest in the remembering process, including, down the line, some contestation among politically interested groups over how the remembering should be concretized.

These are a few of the threads involved in the process of public normalization. More will emerge in the final two sections of this chapter on political and economic aspects of terrorism.

• •

POLITICAL ASPECTS OF RECOVERY

A post-attack development of political solidarity parallels the burst of social solidarity noted above. Citizens experience an increase in trust and support of political leaders, which can endure for long periods of time if a sense of crisis continues and it is perceived that leaders are dealing with the crisis well. The most dramatic evidence of this effect is the report of polls of black Americans in late December 2001, which revealed a figure of 75 percent support for President George W. Bush among a segment of the population that had cast only 10 percent of their votes for him one year earlier. Such support does not last indefinitely, however, as the fate of President George Bush after the Gulf War demonstrates.

Political leadership also pulls together in such times of crisis, particularly if the crisis involves an attack on the nation as a whole. This effect is not necessarily seen in other types of crises—such as an economic collapse of the domestic economy and major political scandals—which typically set off both class and party conflicts.

Partisan politics are quick to return, however, even in areas that have some connection with the crisis. It was less than two months after September 11 when Democrats and Republicans split along recognizable lines over the issue of whether airline security personnel should be federal employees or remain as private-sector employees. By December 2001, the *New York Times*, in summarizing the national situation, quipped that "the Democrats and Republicans are fighting about everything but terrorism" ("This Week in Review," December 23, 2001, p. 1).

Apparently this effect is a general one. In 1689, after the semiforced departure of the Catholic King James II and the succession of William of Orange, a Whig political leader observed that "fear of Popery has united [Whigs and Tories]; when that is over, we shall divide again" (O'Gorman, 1997: 43).

We mention four other political possibilities:

- Tension between the exigencies of national security and the preservation of civil liberties. This tension seems real and perhaps inevitable in times of political crisis. The two sets of considerations pull in opposite directions. Three foci of tension after September 11 were the issues of (a) detention of immigrants, (b) the use of military tribunals for trying apprehended terrorists, and (c) the continuing controversy over the practice — and negative repercussions—of ethnic profiling in checking and searching for suspects. This tension between vigilance and liberty is of special significance and is likely to be a running sore in the context of American democracy, because of the nation's commitment to civil liberties.

- Discrimination against and scapegoating of relevant minority groups in the domestic population, sometimes encouraged or even executed by the government. The negative actions taken against German Americans during World War I and the more drastic measures taken against Japanese Americans in World War II are cases in point. In the present crisis, neither the government nor the populace has turned against Muslim Americans in the same overt way, except for some local incidents. The crisis created uneasiness and ambivalence in that sector of the population, however, despite exhortations for tolerance in government and media circles. A sense of comfort and pride can be gained from the posture of moderation on the part of the government, the press, and the public. It should not be supposed, however, that the issue is permanently closed. In the future, successful terrorist attacks, especially major ones, or evidence or suspicion of terrorist activities on the part of Muslim Americans could quickly turn the picture around and stimulate explosive group antagonisms.

- Confusion of political opposition with lack of patriotism. One aspect of political solidarity and the diminution of partisanship during national crises of the sort now being experienced is that opposition parties and groups extend unusual trust of, and cooperation with, top national leaders. The engine that drives this is patriotism—love of nation. Two features of this unusual type of political situation may make for a muting of political opposition: (a) a temptation of the leaders and party in power to play their political trump card by insinuating or claiming that political opposition is tainted with a lack of loyalty and (b) the tendency for opposition voices to drift toward a self-imposed muteness, out of apprehension that voters in their own districts may also confuse opposition with lack of loyalty. The optimal resolution of these tendencies is the recognition of the right to oppose responsibly and legitimately in the context of an appreciated loyalty to the nation, but this is a matter of delicate equilibrium, not automatically guaranteed.

  • Extremist political movements. An extension of these three tendencies can result in nationally disruptive political movements that evoke accusations of disloyalty in periods of realistic or exaggerated threats. There is nothing inevitable about the development of such movements, but it is worth recalling two disturbing episodes of stereotyping and group punishment in the twentieth century: (a) the red scare of the early 1920s, in which government intimidation and actual raids were carried out in the context of a great national fear of Bolshevism and (b) McCarthyism in the late 1940s and early 1950s, which occurred in the context of a state of high national anxiety over the development of nuclear explosives and weaponry by the Soviet Union and the fall of mainland China to communism in 1948. Both movements, while limited in duration, seriously compromised the civil liberties and livelihood of some citizens, and both left ugly scars on the body politic.

Raising these four possibilities is in no way to predict that any or all will materialize as the nation continues to struggle with its current situation. We cannot unambiguously predict political movements, even though social scientists understand a good deal about the conditions under which movements develop.

· ·

ECONOMIC ASPECTS OF RECOVERY

Some potential terrorist targets are economic in nature. The disruption or destruction of the stock market, the paralysis of credit systems, and the contamination of currency with toxic and infectious agents come to mind. While potentially very disruptive in the short run, these types of attacks—except perhaps the last—are such that reasonably rapid recovery can be envisioned.

Other direct economic consequences are the costs of rebuilding what has been damaged or destroyed. Depending on the scope and success of the attacks, these costs can be very significant. The full cost of replacing the World Trade Center (including compensation for survivors) and the damaged portion of the Pentagon are enormous, as would be the costs of replacing destroyed dams and severely damaged electrical supply systems. Once capital resources are raised and put to work, however, reconstruction projects take on the same stimulating significance for the economy as some public works projects.

Assessment of the indirect and derived economic consequences of terrorist attacks is a more complicated matter, in part because of the great diversity of possible targets. The overall economic losses generated by the September 11 attacks, while evidently severe, are difficult to establish, all the more so because the national economy had already entered a period of downturn. Temporary and selective economic dislocations, however, are readily traceable; some of these were mentioned above. In general, economic dislocations resulting from discrete terrorist activities should be expected to obey the laws of routinization—however slowly in some cases—as people in the affected parts of the economy gradually return to their normally preferred lines of activity and expenditures.

Another economic effect that appears over time in the wake of national traumas is the process of capitalizing on public crisis and turning it in the direction of private gain. The plea on the part of airlines for financial relief is not exactly a case in point, because the losses they suffered after September 11 were genuine; nevertheless, the possibilities of turning relief into gain are always present. The need to gird up for prevention, retaliation against, and aggressive pursuit of terrorism inevitably sets off a scramble for government contracts in relevant parts of the economy. This pattern is observable in wartime situations and was evident throughout the cold war, and it is to be expected to reappear during the coming years. Other, more trivial examples of small-time entrepreneurial activity could also be cited, such as the manufacture and sale of patriotic t-shirts, hats, sweaters, and souvenirs.

The economic question of who pays will be a continuous one. Even under normal circumstances, American politics are fraught with ambiguities and conflicts over the respective costs to be borne by federal, regional, state, and local authorities. The defense against terrorism promises to make the uncertainties even more salient. Given the number and diversity of possible attacks, the prospect of terrorism is simultaneously national, regional, and local. Furthermore, while the fight against terrorism is manifestly a public and governmental responsibility, many if not most of the targets of terrorism are in the private sector. Given all these intersections, who prepares and who pays? More rational and less rational solutions to these dilemmas can be designed, but the nation must expect a significant residue of tugging and hauling, jockeying for position, and resentment of perceived off-loading.

Two final sets of derived consequences of uncertain dimensions also lie on the horizon. The first is the impact of a continuous, quasi-wartime effort on the balance and strength of the American economy. Such an effort will involve significant reallocation of public expenditures and capital among different industrial sectors (especially those connected with defense), the prospect of governmental budgetary deficits, some impact on the pattern of imports and exports, and perhaps a greater sensitivity to periods of inflation.

The second is the prospect of giving lower priority to some expenditures for programs in education, health, welfare, and other areas in consideration of the more urgent demands for military and home defense expenditures. War efforts typically slow the progress of social programs (demands for which often follow wars in a flurry). The quasi-wartime exigencies associated with counterterrorist activities promise to be no exception. It is also possible that the economically relevant aspects of environmental protection will fall from salience as well, unless special efforts are made to sustain them. Environmental efforts involve costs to the nation, and they could come to be seen as competitive with more urgent expenditures.

4 Recommendations for Research

This analysis suggests a number of areas in which systematic theoretical and empirical research—some ongoing, some new—can create, confirm, refine, and reject understandings about terrorism as a social and political phenomenon, thereby improving the knowledge base for efforts to contend with it. As is the case throughout this report, we highlight Islamic-based terrorism, but many of the research recommendations cover a wider range of terrorist activities. We present these suggested areas in the form of a numbered list.

ORIGINS, CHARACTERISTICS, AND DYNAMICS OF TERRORISM

1. To develop individual-level background profiles of terrorists, using as many samples of terrorists as can be made available. Entries in these profiles could include data on family background (parents' occupations or economic circumstances, size of family, place in sibling order), education, job history, political history, circumstances of recruitment and indoctrination into terrorism, and career history as a terrorist. Such research must rely on multiple unrepresentative samples, including populations of detainees, terrorist suspects garnered from intelligence sources, and writings of terrorists themselves if available. Comparisons with like populations—persons engaged in illegal international drug trafficking, members of religious cults and extremist movements—might also prove of some use.

2. To assess the motivational dynamics of terrorists and the characteristics of their value systems. Extremely difficult to

conduct, this kind of research could tap data dealing with past psychological histories of terrorists, attitudes toward authority, religiosity, and history of mental disturbance, as well as psychological measures of narcissism, ambivalence, and different types and levels of psychological commitment to terrorist activities. Information could come from some of the same samples that would yield individual-level background profiles. Also useful would be applications of cognitive analysis in the field of computer science and facets of artificial intelligence to untangle and structure the constituent elements of value structures.

3. To examine the evidence regarding impacts of values on actions, in order to derive knowledge about factors that serve as critical drivers to transform potential or latent terrorists into overt terrorists.

4. To determine the types and range of structures, processes, and organizational careers of terrorist organizations.

- With respect to structure, comparative studies could yield structural typologies of terrorist organizations—hierarchical or flat structure, religious or secular, types of sanctions holding them together, and types of leaders, including level of internal differentiation of leadership. Estimates of organizational effectiveness and vulnerability according to type could also be generated.

- With respect to group processes, empirical study could reveal typical communication processes and breakdowns, bases of internal conflict, competition among leaders, breakdown and restoration of social control, formation of subcliques, coordination of attacks and other operations, conduct of relations with other groups and networks, and modes of contending with pressures from outside, including states in their host societies.

- With respect to the careers of organizations, study could yield knowledge about conditions facilitating the formation of groups; patterns of recruitment; the role of religious and nonreligious leaders; the impact of terrorist success, failure, and inaction on organizational morale and momentum; tendencies to transform into lobbies or political parties; schismatic tendencies and their consequences; and conditions contributing to the stagnation and extinction of terrorist organizations.

- With respect to the power base, it is important to determine the resources available to terrorist organizations as a way of understanding their capabilities in terms of funding, training, information, and refuge.

5. To develop estimates of the probability of selection of different patterns of action and different types of targets by terrorist groups. Factors to be taken into account in generating such estimates include symbolic resonance with the ideological emphases of terrorist organizations (in the Middle East, anti-Christian, anti-Israel, extreme Jewish fundamentalist, antiglobal capitalism, antisecular), terrorists' own thinking about what kinds of events induce terror, their own strategic assessments about what kinds of events are maximally disruptive, the hoped-for political and military effects of attacks, and the degree to which different attacks are spectacular and news-generating. These kinds of estimates will be facilitated by gaining access to and systematizing work on the communication patterns, language, and idioms used by terrorists themselves.

6. To develop through comparative research knowledge about the relevant audiences for terrorism and modes of communicating with these audiences as a way of determining the impacts of audience on the content of communication.

7. To elucidate the effects of host states harboring or giving rise to terrorists, in terms of the impact of type of state (according to wealth, poverty, and political culture) and state policies (support, benign neglect, attempts to domesticate or coopt, political repression) on the sources of terrorist groups, their potential for recruitment, and the careers and effectiveness of terrorist organizations

8. To survey and monitor demographic trends in fertility, mortality, and nuptiality in societies likely to develop terrorist activity; to draw out implications of these patterns for their potential to generate economic and educational development and to produce classes of idle, poverty-stricken, and frustrated youth.

9. To develop further work on the cultural and social backgrounds to terrorism, especially different types of Islamic revivalism. This could be broken down into subtopics, such as transnational or global Islamic movements; linguistic, cultural, and contextual factors; local or regional movements; conditions that promote different types of revivalism; implications for Muslim communities in the United States; and case studies of religious-based terrorism in particular countries (Islamic as well as non-Islamic).

10. To conduct historical and comparative research on the effects of Western economic, political, cultural, military, and

foreign policy activities on less developed countries—by categories of countries and types of activities—as well as the short-term impact on the patterns of terrorist activities. Such research is difficult to conduct with reliability and objectivity, first, because of the limited theoretical foundations to guide such work; second, because it is difficult to isolate and trace these consequences through the fabric of the affected societies; and third, because the research topics themselves are ideologically loaded and lie at the basis of debates and political divisions in American society. It is also important to examine the current influences across developing countries—shaped by common historical experiences with the West—that may be used to encourage the diffusion of terrorism.

11. Cutting across all the above types of research is the methodological need to systematize and allow ease of access to different types of data and databases—such as these exist—that may be related to different facets of terrorism. These tasks are formidable because many of these data appear in different languages, are gathered for a great diversity of purposes, and are not immediately comparable with one another.

• •

RESPONSES TO TERRORISM

12. To evaluate warning systems. Comparative empirical studies of past disaster and terrorist situations should attempt to evaluate the respective consequences of effective warnings, failures to warn, miswarnings (false alarms), and overwarning.

13. To monitor immediate responses to disasters. Most disasters are both sudden and ephemeral, and immediate responses give way quickly to a wide variety of recovery and rebuilding activities. Relevant research agencies (universities, think tanks, government) should establish the capacity to move quickly to the scene and study immediate responses while they are occurring. Most research on short-term disaster responses relies on hastily assembled journalistic reports and after-the-fact accounts based of recollections by participants. Both sources are subject to selectivity and distortion. Teams of behavioral and social science researchers, collecting data on the spot and analyzing them in the context of established knowledge about disaster situations, would supplement and probably improve

on existing ways of generating information and understanding. Some universities have a tradition of fire brigade research; efforts should be made to expand and systematize it.

14. To track group differences in response to crises. Most thinking about preparedness, warning, and response rests on the assumption of an undifferentiated community or public. Research on disasters, however, has revealed that individuals and groups differ both in readiness and response according to previous disaster experience, ethnic and minority status, knowledge of the language, level of education, level of economic resources, and gender (Tierney et al., 2001). Research on these and other differences should be extended and deepened and taken into account when designing systems of preparedness, warning, and response to terrorist attacks and other disaster situations.

15. To evaluate the behavior of agencies of response to crisis. There should be a deepening of research—basic, comparative, and applied—on the structure of agencies designated as responsible for dealing with attacks and other disasters, on the optimal patterns of information dissemination and communication among them, and on the most effective strategies of coordination and self-correcting of coordination under extreme conditions. Research should also focus on the origins and consequences of organizational failure, miscommunication, lack of coordination, and jurisdictional conflict and squabbling.

16. To evaluate the practice of ethnic profiling. Advocated as both a necessary and effective method of identifying and apprehending terrorist suspects, ethnic profiling raises both methodological and policy issues. A scientific review should be made of its methodological underpinnings, including implied statistical assumptions and possible fallacies. In addition, the practice of profiling raises many questions about intrusiveness on civil rights and possible boomerang political effects in affected groups. A starting point for research might be an examination of scientific issues and political effects in affected groups. Such a study group could consult not only the literature on terrorism but also that in other areas (e.g., police arrest practices, housing discrimination) in which the issue has emerged.

17. To assess both short-term and long-term group responses to terrorism and terrorist attacks in terms of attitudes and opinions. Questions would include the attitudinal consequences of living in prolonged situations of heightened anxiety, as well as

the dynamics of the balance between tendency toward national and community solidarity (tending to diminish group difference and conflict) and the tendency for fault lines dividing groups along ethnic, religious, and political dimensions to become more salient. In the current atmosphere, special attention should be given to the situation of Muslim Americans—blacks, Asians, and Arabs—who consider themselves part of the nation's demographic, cultural, and political fabric but who have experienced considerable stress in the context of national reactions to terrorist activities emanating from the states of origin of some of these citizens. This last line of research could be supplemented by comparative work on ethnic, especially Muslim, minorities in European countries, including France, Germany, and the United Kingdom, where the forces shaping the national and ethnic loyalties differ from those in the United States.

18. To develop sequential and cumulative analyses of terrorist events. Because terrorist attacks tend to be sudden, surprising, and of short duration, they are usually regarded as discrete events. In reality, however, they build on one another, and any new attack or attacks is read, variably by different groups, in the context of the past history of such events. One of the interpretative frames of reacting to the attack on the World Trade Center, for example, was the memory of the unsuccessful effort to destroy it by bombing in 1993. Reactions to anthrax episodes were strongly conditioned—and exaggerated—because they occurred so soon in the wake of September 11. The whole history of mutual terrorism between Palestine and Israel is a history of stored memories of many past occurrences, evoked when new attacks occur and referred to continuously by both sides. Historical research on the interrelated sequencing of reactions, interpretations, and memories of terrorist events would deepen theoretical and empirical understanding of those phenomena. Conceptual models, such as path dependency (employed in economics, political science, and other fields) and the logic of "value added," would offer guidelines to framing and conducting this kind of research. Formal modeling of these kinds of sequences should also be explored.

References

Abootalebi, Ali R.
  1999 Islam, Islamists, and Democracy. [Online]. Available: http://meria.idc.ac.il/journal/1999/issue1/jvol3no1in.html [Accessed June 26, 2002].

Alam, Shah
  2000 Conservatives, Liberals and the Struggle Over Iranian Politics. [Online]. Available: http://www.ciaonet.org/olj/sa/sa_jun00als01.html [Accessed June 26, 2002].

Ansell, Christopher K.
  2002 *Schism and Solidarity in Social Movements: The Politics of Labor in the French Third Republic.* New York: Cambridge University Press.

Arquilla, John, and David Ronfeldt
  2001 *Networks and Netwars: The Future of Terror, Crime, and Militancy.* Santa Monica, CA: RAND.

Carley, K., J. Lee, and D. Krackhardt
  2001 Destabilizing networks. *Connections* 24(3): 31-34.

Crenshaw, Martha
  1981 The causes of terrorism. *Comparative Politics* 13:379-399.
  1985 An organizational approach to the analysis of political terrorism. *Orbis* 29(3):465-489.
  1987 Theories of terrorism: Instrumental and organizational approaches. *Journal of Strategic Studies (Special Issue)* 10(4):13-31.
  2001 Terrorism. Pp. 15604-06 in *International Encyclopedia of the Social and Behavioral Sciences,* Vol. 23, Neil J. Smelser and Paul B. Baltes (eds.). Oxford: Elsevier.

Della Porta, Donatella
  1992 Introduction: On individual motivations in underground political organizations. Pp. 3-28 in *Social Movements and Violence: Participation in Underground Organizations,* D. Donatella (ed.). Greenwich, CT: JAI Press.

Dow, Kirstin, Patrice Burns, and Susan L. Cutter
  1999 To stay or leave: Residents' evaluation of hurricane evacuation warnings. Pp. 107- 114 in *Papers and Proceedings of the Applied Geography Conference*, Vol 22, F. Andrew Schoolmaster (ed.). Charlotte, NC: University of South Carolina Hazards Research Lab.

Dow, Kirstin, and Susan L. Cutter
  1998 Crying wolf: Repeat responses to hurricane evacuation orders. *Coastal Management* 26: 237-252.

2000 Public orders and personal opinions: Household strategies for hurricane risk assessment. *Environmental Hazards* 2(4):143-155.

Erickson, B.
1981 Secret societies and social structures. *Social Forces* 60(1):188-210

Gallie, W. B.
1956 Essentially contested concepts. Pp. 157-98 in *Proceedings of the Philosophical Society*, Vol. 51. London: Harrison and Sons, Ltd.

Hamzeh, A. Nizar
1997 Islamism in Lebanon: A Guide. [Online]. Available: http://meria.idc.ac.il/journal/1997/issue3/jvol1no3in.html [Accessed June 26, 2002].

Hoffman, Bruce
1998 *Inside Terrorism*. New York: Columbia University Press.

Johnson, Larry C.
2001 The future of terrorism. *American Behavioral Scientist* 44(6):894-913.

Juergensmeyer, Mark
2000 *Terror in the Mind of God: The Global Rise of Religious Violence*. Berkeley: University of California Press.

Kerbs, V. E.
2001 Mapping networks of terrorist cells. *Connections* 24(3): 43-52.

Lewis, Bernard
2002 *What Went Wrong? Western Impact and Middle Eastern Response*. New York: Oxford University Press.

Library of Congress
1999 *The Sociology and Psychology of Terrorism: Who Becomes a Terrorist and Why?* Report prepared under an Interagency Agreement by the Federal Research Division, Hudson, Rex. Washington, D.C.: Library of Congress. [Online]. Available: http://www.loc.gov/rr/frd/Sociology-Psychology%20of%20Terrorism.htm [Accessed: June 26, 2002]

Maddy-Weitzman, Bruce
1996 The Islamic challenge in North Africa. *Terrorism and Political Violence,* 8(2):171-188 (Summer).

McCauley, Clark
In press Psychological issues in understanding terrorism and the response to terrorism. In *The Psychology of Terrorism,* Christopher Stout (ed.). Westport, CT: Greenwood Publishing.
2002 Understanding the 9/11 perpetrators: crazy, lost in hate, or martyred? In *History Behind the Headlines*, Vol. 5, N. Matuszak (ed.). Gale Publishing Group.

McCauley, C.R., and M.E. Segal
1987 Social psychology of terrorist groups. In *Group Processes and Intergroup Relations*, Vol. 9 of *Annual Review of Social and Personality Psychology*, C. Hendrick, ed. Beverly Hills: Sage.

Mead, Margaret
1965 *And Keep Your Powder Dry: An Anthropologist Looks at American Life.* New York: Morrow. [1942]

Mileti, D.S., C. Fitzpatrick, and B.C. Farhar
1990 *Risk Communication and Public Response to the Parkfield Earthquake Prediction Experiment.* Fort Collins, CO: Hazards Assessment Laboratory and Assessment Laboratory and Department of Sociology, Colorado State University.

Mooney, J.
1896 The ghost-dance religion and the Sioux outbreak of 1890. *Fourteenth Annual Report of the Bureau of Ethnology*. Washington, DC: U.S. Government Printing Office.

National Research Council
2002 *Making the Nation Safer: The Role of Science and Technology in Countering Terrorism*. Committee on Science and Technology for Countering Terrorism. Washington, DC: National Academies Press.
In press *Discouraging Terrorism: Some Implications of 9/11*. Committee on Understanding Terrorists to Deter Terrorism. Neil J. Smelser and Faith Mitchell, eds. Washington, DC: The National Academies Press.

National Science and Technology Council.
2000 *Effective Disaster Warnings*. Subcommittee on Natural Disaster Reduction, Committee on Environment and Natural Resources. Report of the Working Group on Natural Disaster Information Systems, Office of the President of the United States. Washington, DC: U.S. Government Printing Office.

O'Gorman, Frank
1997 *The Long Eighteenth Century: British Political and Social History 1688-1832*. London: Arnold Press.

Paulhus, D.L., P.D. Trapnell, and D. Chen
1999 Birth order effects on personality and achievement within families. *Psychological Science* 10(6):482-488.

Post, Jerrold M.
1990 Terrorist psycho-logic: Terrorist behavior as a product of psychological forces. Pp. 25-42 in *Origins of Terrorism: Psychologies, Ideologies, Theologies, States of Mind*, Walter Reich (ed.). Washington, DC: Woodrow Wilson Center Press.
2001 The Mind of the Terrorist: Individual and Group Psychology of Terrorist Behavior. Testimony prepared for the Sub-Committee on Emerging Threats and Capabilities, Senate Armed Services Committee, Nov. 15.

Quarentelli, Enrico L.
1977 Panic behavior: Some empirical observations. Pp. 336-50 in *Human Responses to Tall Buildings*. Stroudsberg, PA: Dowden, Hutchinson, and Post.

Roudi, Farzaneh
2002 Population Trends and Challenges in the Middle East and North Africa. Washington, DC: Population Reference Bureau. Available: http://www.prb.org/Template.cfm?Section=By_Topic&template=/Ecommerce/Topic.cfm&TopicID=48 [Accessed June 19, 2002].

Rubin, Barnett R.
2002 *The Fragmentation of Afghanistan: State Formation and Collapse in the International System*. Second edition. New Haven, CT: Yale University Press.

Ruby, C.L.
2002 Are terrorists mentally deranged? *Analyses of Social Issues and Public Policy* 2:15-26.
2002 The definition of terrorism. *Analyses of Social Issues and Public Policy* 2:9-14.

Schiller, David
2001 A battlegroup divided: The Palestinian fedayeen. Pp. 90-108 in *Inside Terrorist Organizations*, David Rappoport (ed.). London: Frank Cass.

Schmid, Alex P., Albert J. Jongman, et al.
  1988   *Political Terrorism: A New Guide to Actors, Authors, Concepts, Data Bases, Theories, and Literature.* New Brunswick, NJ: Transaction Books.
Sivan, Emmanuel
  1997   Why Radical Muslims Aren't Taking Over Governments. [Online.] Available: http://www.meforum.org/meq/dec97/toc.shtml [Accessed June 26, 2002].
Skinner, G.W.
  1992   Family Process and Political Process in Modern Chinese History. Seek a Loyal Subject in a Filial Son: Family Roots of Political Orientation in Chinese Society. Sponsored by the Institute of Modern History, Academia Sinica; Department of History, University of California, Davis; Chian Ching-kuo Foundation for International Scholarly Exchange, Taipeh, Republic of China.
Slotkin, James S.
  1956   *The Peyote Religion.* Glencoe, IL: The Free Press.
Smelser, Neil J.
  1962   *Theory of Collective Behavior.* New York: The Free Press.
Sprinzak, Ehud
  1990   The psychopolitical formation of extreme left terrorism in a democracy: The case of the Weathermen. Pp. 65-85 in *Origins of Terrorism: Psychologies, Ideologies, Theologies, States of Mind*, Walter Reich (ed.). Washington, DC: Woodrow Wilson Center Press.
  2001   The lone gunmen: The global war on terrorism faces a new brand of enemy. *Foreign Policy* 127:72-73.
Sulloway, Frank
  1996   *Born to Rebel: Birth Order, Family Dynamics, and Creative Lives.* New York: Pantheon.
Takeyh, Ray
  2002   Two cheers from the Islamic world. *Foreign Policy* 128:70-71 (January/February).
Tierney, Kathleen J., Michael K. Lindell, and Ronald W. Perry (eds.)
  2001   *Facing the Unexpected: Disaster Preparedness and Response in the United States.* Washington, DC: Joseph Henry Press.
U.S. Department of State
  1988   *Patterns of Global Terrorism.* Washington, DC: U.S. Department of State.
U.S. Strategic Bombing Survey
  1947   *The Effects of Strategic Bombing on German Morale.* Vol. I. Washington, DC: U.S. Government Printing Office.
Voll, John O.
  1994   Fundamentalism in the Sunni Arab world: Egypt and the Sudan. Pp. 345-402 in *Fundamentalisms Observed*, Martin E. Marty and R. Scott Appleby (eds.). Chicago: University of Chicago Press.
Wallace, Anthony F.C.
  1956   *Human Behavior in Extreme Situations: A Survey of the Literature and Suggestions for Further Research.* Disaster Study Number 1, a paper for the Committee on Disaster Studies of the Division of Anthropology and Psychology. Washington, DC: National Academy Press.
Wolfenstein, Martha
  1957   *Disaster: A Psychological Essay.* Glencoe, IL: The Free Press and the Falcon's Wing Press.

World Bank
    2002 GNI per capita 2000.   Available: http://worldbank.org/data/
        quickreference/quickref.html [Accessed June 19, 2002].
Worsley, Peter
    1957 *The Trumpet Shall Sound: A Study of Cargo Cults in Melanesia.* London:
        MacGibbon and Key.
Zartman, I. William
    1995 *Collapsed States: The Disintegration and Restoration of Legitimate Author-
        ity.* Boulder, CO: L. Rienner Publishers.
Zweigenhaft, R.I., and J. Von Ammon
    2000 Birth order and civil disobedience: A test of Sulloway's "Born to
        Rebel" hypothesis. *The Journal of Psychology* 140(5):624-627.

A Dimensions of Terrorism: Actors, Actions, Consequences

Eugene A. Hammel

Note: All three of the following major dimensions are complex and divide into subdimensions. Many are continua, not discretely dividable. At the lowest level (i, ii, iii, etc.), the outline gives some points on those continua, sometimes with empirical examples.

I. Actors.
    A. Perpetrators.
        1. Identification and visibility.
            a. Invisible, dispersed, cell-like, even unidentified (Pan Am 103 perpetrators before they were identified, Unabomber, Al Qaeda).
            b. Identified, well known (Hamas, Hezbollah, Sendero Luminoso, ETA, similar groups claiming responsibility credibly).
        2. Organization.
            a. Cell-like, diffuse networks with low connectivity—no one knows the whole network (Al Qaeda, Weathermen, underground Communists, some Ku Klux Klan or white supremacist networks).
            b. Identifiable states (Iran, Libya), but not always organized or coherent (Somalia, early Libya).
        3. Belief system.
            a. Source of inspiration or legitimation.
                i. Purely anarchist, violence for its own sake, as an aesthetic experience (Sorel, Sartre, Bakunin, Nechayev).
                ii. Religiously inspired, cult-like, fundamentalist, absolutist, millenarian, messianic (Mahdists, Crusaders, Al Qaeda, other Islamist movements).

iii. Ethnically inspired (ethnic cleansing in Bosnia, Kurdish separatists, ETA).

iv. Politically inspired, even if with millenarian overtones (Communism, Nazism).

b. Instrumentality (closely correlated with type of legitimation).

i. Not instrumental—no negotiations because God has ordained their goals and behavior (e.g., Al Qaeda), or simply glorifying violence (some anarchists).

ii. Highly instrumental, negotiating for clearly defined objectives, (e.g. IRA, ETA, KLA).

B. Victims.

1. National identity.

a. United States.

b. Allies of United States.

c. Neutral countries.

d. Opponents of United States.

2. Connection to the United States ("innocence").

a. Bystanders.

b. Workers.

c. Off-duty military, public safety personnel.

d. Corporate leaders.

e. On-duty military, public safety personnel.

f. Government leaders, diplomats.

C. Third parties.

1. Same as perpetrators (organized war between states, e.g., Pearl Harbor).

2. Sponsors of perpetrators (Iran, elements of Saudi Arabia, early Libyan terrorism).

3 Willing hosts of perpetrators (Libya, Afghanistan).

4. Unwilling hosts of perpetrators (Somalia).

5. Collaborators (some French, possibly some British, Muslims).

6. Sympathizers (some U.S. Muslims re: U.S. support of Israel).

7. Dupes (some coreligionists, disaffected persons, etc.).

8. Unknowingly penetrated by perpetrators (Hamburg, South Florida).

II. Actions.

A. Mechanism of attack.

1. Physical.

a. Objects (ramming, etc.).

b. Explosives.

c. Nuclear.

d. Other energy forms (laser, radio, electromagnetic field).

  2. Chemical.

  3. Biological.

B. Nature of target.

  1. People.

    a. Individuals.

    b. Groups.

  2. Organizations.

    a. Government.

    b. Corporate.

    c. Other public organizations (schools, hospitals, etc.).

C. Degree of violence.

  1. Nonviolent (protest marches, strikes, civil disobedience).

  2. Nondamaging, symbolic (burning effigies, flags, draft cards, etc.).

  3. Mild (breaking windows).

  4. Moderate (computer attacks).

  5. Extreme (murder, arson, deadly contamination).

D. Scope of violence.

  1. Highly localized (individual), e.g., a single assassination.

  2. Multiple simultaneous or co-incidentally local, e.g., several assassinations or attacks on buildings or air flights.

  3. Widespread and continuous, e.g., a smallpox epidemic.

E. Degree of surprise.

  1. Total.

  2. Accurately warned.

  3. Inaccurately or falsely warned.

III. Consequences.

A. Physical damage to infrastructure, e.g., bridges, buildings, electrical grids, including communication systems, computer networks, software, etc.

B. Biological damage to people, animals, plants, e.g., epidemics, epizootics, epiphytics.

C. Environmental damage.

D. Psychological damage, e.g., panic, suspicion, loss of trust in government.

E. Social disruption, e.g., ethnic conflict, class warfare.

F. Economic disruption, e.g., suspension of trade, banking, supply, etc.

A number of diverse implications follow from such attempts to classify disasters:

1. With some arbitrariness, the attacks on the World Trade Center and the Pentagon building on September 11 can be classified as a physical attack (II.A) by a religiously inspired (I.A.3.ii) organization (I.A.2). It was an attack based on total surprise (II.E) and involved both physical damage (III.A) and harm to people, who included corporate executives (I.B.2.d), workers (I.B.2,d), and some bystanders (I.B.2.a). Most victims were U.S. citizens (I.B.1.a) but some others were killed as well.

2. Some attacks that differ from the September 11 attack (e.g., bioterrorism) can be equally or more dangerous to the security of the country and its population. Some others that perhaps differ in major ways on some dimensions may be less dangerous, down to the mere nuisance level, and could be tolerated or handled routinely as common criminality, or as acts of persons perhaps legally insane, or as those of people exercising their political and civil rights. It is important to examine what these variations might be in order to estimate what kinds of resources must be devoted to the defense against terrorism and how they should be deployed.

3. Violence may be more or less extreme; less extreme violence is cheaper and simpler to exert. Violence may not be catastrophic but only intended to demonstrate the continued threat of catastrophe and thus keep terrorists visible and the target population in a state of terror or at least uncertainty. It may be applied just to prove that the opponents are still a force to be reckoned with. It may be applied with warning to generate even more panic, and it may be warned without actually being executed to create further confusion and uncertainty at even lower short-term cost to the terrorists. Indeed, the warnings of terrorist attack may actually come from U.S. officials, based on tips or evidence of varying credibility. Terrorist threats may be as effective as terrorist *acts*.

4. Attacks could target less "innocent" persons, for ex-

ample, government officials, military personnel, or police on duty. It is important to note that the definition of "innocent" applied by the target country may not be the same definition of "innocent" applied by the terrorists. Merely being a citizen of or a worker in the United States may strip the victim of innocence in the eyes of the terrorist.

5.   Attacks can also be directed at allies of the United States, partners in the coalition against terrorism, or coreligionist states of the terrorists, even the countries from which the terrorists come, if they are regarded as complicit. It could be directed at countries that were not allies or even coalition partners. However, the exercise of terror against a country unfriendly to the United States (like North Korea, Iraq, Somalia) or now marginally supportive of it (like Libya) might be construed in the United States not as terror but rather as a liberation movement. This minor stretching of the definition suggests that the idea of terrorism has a distinct, political, "us-them" characteristic. A definition of terror that is based on who gets hit undermines any general attempts to delegitimize it.

6.   Common definitions of the "new terrorism" are problematic. Some terrorists can be domestic but may have characteristics otherwise identical to those at the core of our concern. That is, domestic terrorists' ideology may be apocryphal, they may use extreme violence, they may target innocent persons, they may destroy in order to protest what they see as a satanic or repressive culture or government. The bombing of the Murrah building in Oklahoma City, the existence of armed, extremist, Nazi-like groups, the bombing of abortion clinics and assassination of their personnel are examples. The defense against terror should not exclude such dangers simply because they are homegrown.

7.   The terrorists at the core of our concern have been Muslim and Islamist. It is important to realize that there are Christians and Jews inside and outside the United States who have exactly the same objections to U.S. elite and popular culture, especially to secular humanism, tolerance of alternative sexual preferences, reproductive rights, equal status for women, tolerance of religious and ethnic differences, etc. Some such groups feel oppressed, and some feel betrayed. Some of these objections are shared, in whole or in part, even by people in the United States who are atheists. Ideological discomfort or moral outrage need not be strictly religious. What is important is appreciation

of the perception, by antagonists, that American society is morally anarchic and has spun totally out of control. It is not just some Muslims who think that, and, it is not just some Muslims who would act on it.

8. Guru-like figures are common in a variety of religions, including both Western and Eastern ones, especially in cult-like offshoots like the Peoples' Temple of Jim Jones, the Branch Davidians, and others. Rigid pastoral control has also been typical of some now-mainstream Protestant sects. Cynical exploitation of members, as among the Hare Krishna or the followers of Sun Myung Moon, is common and often takes the form of sexual exploitation.

9. The scope of the goals is a function of the apocryphal vision. Because the goals are utopian, foreordained, and sanctified, they cannot be negotiated. Such visions of utopia are extremely common in religions that emphasize an afterlife. They are also typical of some millenarian and apocalyptic political movements, such as communism, nazism, and (to a lesser extent), fascism. These political cults differ from millenarian religions principally in the absence of a deity, although some may hold their leader to be a messiah.

B Committee on Science and Technology for Countering Terrorism

LEWIS M. BRANSCOMB (*Co-Chair*), Center for Science and International Affairs (emeritus), John F. Kennedy School of Government, Harvard University

RICHARD D. KLAUSNER (*Co-Chair*), Case Institute of Health, Science and Technology

JOHN D. BALDESCHWIELER, Division of Chemistry and Chemical Engineering, California Institute of Technology, Pasadena California

BARRY R. BLOOM, School of Public Health, Harvard University

L. PAUL BREMER III, Marsh and McLennan Companies, Inc., Washington, D.C.

WILLIAM F. BRINKMAN, Lucent Technologies (retired), Murray Hill, New Jersey

ASHTON B. CARTER, School of Science and International Affairs and Preventive Defense Project, John F. Kennedy School of Government, Harvard University

CHARLES B. CURTIS, Nuclear Threat Initiative, Washington, D.C.

MORTIMER L. DOWNEY III, PBConsult, Washington, D.C.

RICHARD L. GARWIN, IBM Thomas J. Watson Research Center (emeritus), New York, New York

PAUL H. GILBERT, Parsons Brinckerhoff International, Inc., Seattle, Washington

M.R.C. GREENWOOD, Office of the Chancellor, University of California, Santa Cruz

MARGARET A. HAMBURG, Biological Programs, Nuclear Threat Initiative, Washington, D.C.

WILLIAM HAPPER, Department of Physics, Princeton University

JOHN L. HENNESSY, President, Stanford University

JOSHUA LEDERBERG, Sackler Foundation, The Rockefeller University

THOMAS C. SCHELLING, School of Public Affairs, University of Maryland

MAXINE F. SINGER, President, Carnegie Institution of Washington, Washington, D.C.

NEIL J. SMELSER, Department of Sociology (emeritus), University of California, Berkeley

PHILIP M. SMITH, McGeary & Smith, Washington, D.C.

P. ROY VAGELOS, Regeneron Pharmaceuticals, Inc., Bedminster, New Jersey

VINCENT VITTO, The Charles Stark Draper Laboratory, Inc., Cambridge, Massachussetts

GEORGE M. WHITESIDES, Department of Chemistry, Harvard University

R. JAMES WOOLSEY, Booz Allen Hamilton, McLean, Virginia